Hostage Bound, Hostage Free

Hostage Bound
Hostage Free

Ben and Carol Weir
with Dennis Benson

The Westminster Press
Philadelphia

Book design by Gene Harris

First edition

The Christian Herald Association, Inc., Book Club Edition of this work is published by arrangement with The Westminster Press, 925 Chestnut Street, Philadelphia, Pennsylvania 19107.

PRINTED IN THE UNITED STATES OF AMERICA

A four-page section of photographs follows page 99.

Library of Congress Cataloging-in-Publication Data

Weir, Ben, 1923–
    Hostage bound, hostage free.

    1. Weir, Ben, 1923–   —Captivity, 1984–1985.
2. Weir, Carol, 1924–   3. Hostages—Lebanon—
Biography. 4. Hostages—United States—Biography.
I. Weir, Carol, 1924–   II. Benson, Dennis C.
III. Title.
DS87.2.W 1987   956.92′044′0922 [B]   86–34004
ISBN 0–664–21322–7

To our children
Christine, Susan, and John
who are very much a part of this story
and in memory of the beautiful life of Ann
who meant so much to us all

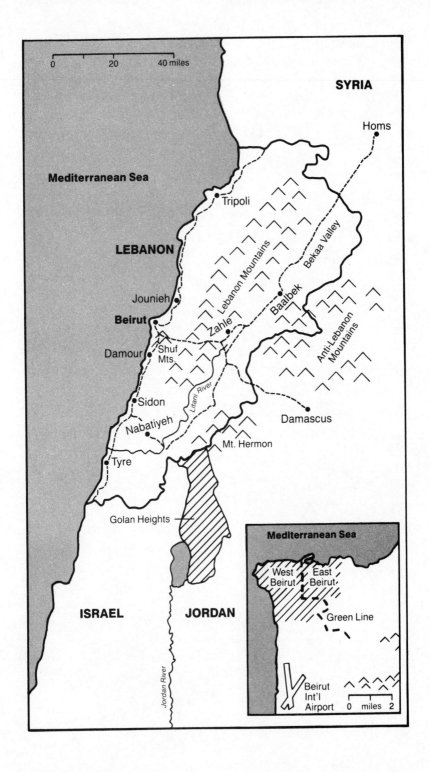

There was only darkness. The blindfold over my eyes completely blocked out the light. I was lying on my back on a low bed. The unforgettable sound of adhesive tape being unwound from its roll filled the room. Strong hands wrapped this wide packing tape around my head, over my forehead, eyes, and mouth, and around my neck. Only a small space over my nostrils was left open.

Next, my arms and hands were held close to my sides, and the tape was wound slowly around my whole body, starting with the legs and moving up past my shoulders. I was being totally encased. Someone forced me into a sitting position, and another layer of tape was wound around my neck, under my chin, and over the top of my head. I was a hostage bound.

Arms lifted me from the bed and carried me out. My body was pushed into a long narrow container. I heard a lid being closed and bolted over me. I could feel solid metal through my shoeless feet. I raised my head a few inches and struck a solid metal top. I moved my hips from side to side as best I could and found metal on either side. I lay there like a corpse in a coffin.

I heard an engine start, gears grind, and a metal door open. Only when it lurched forward did I suddenly realize I was on a truck. To add to my terror, I could now smell heavy exhaust fumes coming up through the floor of the truck body. I must be right over the tailpipe. Already I was breathing heavily through my nose.

God, I prayed, *don't let the air passages clog!*

1

*"Be quiet. Don't make any noise.
If you do, I'll kill you."*

How in the world did a Presbyterian missionary who had been
working quietly in Lebanon for thirty-one years end up in such a
situation?

Only a few hours earlier, my wife, Carol, and I had stepped from
our apartment into the streets of West Beirut, on our way to a meeting. The morning of May 8, 1984, blended beauty with harshness. On
that bright spring day in the Muslim section of the city, the sounds
of birds coming from the untended garden plot next to our apartment building contrasted with the angry growl of distant explosions.
Citizens of wartorn Beirut had learned to move carefully when they
were out of doors. Many armed groups roamed at will, expressing
their anger and frustration in street fighting.

We were headed on foot for the Near East School of Theology, an
ecumenical seminary several blocks away. The day before, during a
meeting there of the Board of Managers, I had heard for hours the
sound of explosions and the occasional chatter of machine guns
around the city. Tension almost crackled in the air.

Toward the end of the afternoon, a somber note had been struck
when Dr. Ray H. Kiely, our interim president, suddenly announced
that he would be resigning at the end of his first year. He and his wife,
Martha, had instilled a sense of community and stability in the life
of the seminary. Now Ray felt he had contributed what he could and
should leave.

One of the board members, Hovhannes Karjian, an Armenian pastor, and I wanted to try to persuade Ray to stay on as president for
the coming year, so we decided to get together early the next morning, before the board resumed its work. I had promised to contact
Hovhannes by phone that evening, even though my telephone at
home was not working, so after supper I walked in the half-light to
my office two short blocks from our apartment. I tried repeatedly to

put my call through, but without success. The phones simply weren't working anywhere.

Finally, with a sense of frustration, I locked my office door and started out of the building. It was dark; the streetlights had been destroyed long ago. I had barely reached the street and closed the iron gate when heavy fire from automatic weapons erupted all around me. I could hear the sounds of rocket-propelled grenades, antiaircraft fire, and submachine guns coming from every direction.

My first thought was that the Lebanese civil war had broken out all over again, and the fighting had suddenly reached our neighborhood. I ran to the cover of a nearby building whose second story jutted out over the sidewalk. No one was on the street. Should I stay there or go back to my office?

Then, as I watched a fountain of glowing tracer bullets in the night sky, I realized what was happening on this dark street in Beirut. This was not a battle but a celebration!

That fit in with the news I had just heard over the transistor radio in my office. After long debate, Nabih Berri, a prominent Shiite Muslim leader, had accepted a ministerial position in the new cabinet of the Lebanese government. Perhaps this not only would give more political power to the Shiite community but would help a deadlocked government begin to function.

The shooting into the air continued unabated. I waited for a while, remembering that, on previous occasions like this, some stray bullets had showered down around me. Finally, I carefully made my way home. As I went along, I could hear spent bullets thud against the stone walls and pavements.

Before we left the apartment the next morning, I gave Carol our residence permits, the documents that the Lebanese government requires of all foreigners living in the country. Each year they are to be renewed on January 1, but we had been away from Lebanon on furlough until the beginning of March. As soon as we returned to the Middle East, I had begun the process of renewal. It proved to be a lengthy one. During March and April, I had made thirteen trips on foot to government offices to move the procedure along. Each time I had to appear in person. Two of the trips were across the fortified Green Line, which separates Christian East Beirut from the predominantly Muslim western part of the city.

Now, in early May, I had the residence permits in my hands. Since it was always possible for them to be stolen or lost, I asked Carol to have them photocopied at the seminary. It was providential that I was not carrying them when we went out that morning. Carol would

have need of her residence permit, and I was about to become a man
without identity.

At the door I paused briefly, considering the possible dangers of
going out into the street once again. But Carol and I both felt the
meeting at the seminary was important.

We had gone only a short way when a car pulled up from behind
us and stopped. Two men got out and said something. The words
were not clear, but I assumed they were in English. "What do you
want?" I asked one of the men.

I hardly understood his response. "I want you!"

With that he grabbed my arm and started pulling me toward the
car. Carol and I realized at the same moment that this was a kidnap
attempt. She began screaming, and I yelled for help.

I tried to resist, but the man was much younger and stronger than
I was. He twisted my necktie and pulled me toward the car. I braced
my hands on both sides of the open back door, but he gave me a
tremendous shove from behind and forced me into the back seat.

A man with a black beard jumped into the front passenger seat and
pointed an automatic pistol at my head while the driver put the car
in motion. The man who had seized me forced me down on the floor
of the car and pulled a sack over me, keeping his hand on my back.
By now the car was speeding along. I realized I was at the mercy of
my assailants, helpless, unable to escape.

Frightening thoughts raced through my mind. What was going to
happen to me? Would I be killed? Would I be held for ransom?
Tortured? And why me? Did they want someone else and take me
by mistake?

I felt completely powerless, like so many hundreds of Lebanese
who have themselves been captured and taken away. I had read
about such kidnappings frequently and had talked to distraught relatives of the kidnap victims many times.

Well, I said to myself, now it's happening to me. It's not a story in
the paper, it's for real. This is a new experience. Now I'll know what
it's like to be kidnapped.

Despite this mental pep talk, I couldn't help worrying: Here I am,
a gun at my head, unable to do anything for myself. I can't get free.
I can't even call out for help. I don't know what lies ahead. I may be
hurt, even killed.

Yet I was guided by a deep assurance. I felt that I was supported,
cradled, in the dependable arms of God. He knew where I was. He
knew the men who had me in their control. He was aware of where
the car was going and of what lay ahead. I could count on God. So
in spite of my anxiety and fear, I began to relax.

Cramped as I was, I moved my feet into a more comfortable position and cradled my head in my arms. This reminded me that I had my glasses on, so I took them off and put them in an inside pocket of my jacket. I was glad they were still intact.

I tried to figure out the direction in which we were moving. The car inched through the busy, crowded streets of West Beirut, stop and go, stop and go. The driver was anxious, wanting to move ahead, swearing in Arabic at the cars in front of him. The man next to me kept saying no one was following. I heard a policeman's whistle nearby and hoped to God he would stop and check the car. But we moved ahead and he was left behind.

Soon the car began to travel more quickly, going around corners and then speeding up for short stretches. We stopped again, waiting for traffic to clear. Again curses from the driver filled the car. Then we moved ahead, made a wide turn, and raced over a hard-surfaced road. After perhaps ten minutes or so, the car began bouncing over rougher terrain. I suspected that we were now entering the southern suburbs of the city—the poorer area of Muslim West Beirut. Was this where I was to be kept?

My disturbing questions came back to me. What will happen to me? Will I be held for ransom? Will they physically hurt me? Will they accuse me of working for the CIA?

We bounced on for perhaps another ten or fifteen minutes. Then the driver began to talk to the other two men in a more relaxed fashion. We must be nearing our destination. He called to me, "Hey, man, how are you? You okay?"

A new emotion was growing within me: anger and indignation. What right had they to take me from Carol and my work? Kidnapping is a violation of human rights and against the religion of Islam. I had served the personal and social needs of hundreds of Lebanese people during the past thirty-one years in this beloved country. How dare they consider me the enemy? I said nothing in response to his question. I would be stubbornly silent. My muteness would be my resistance.

After another five minutes or so the car came to a sudden halt. The driver said in a low voice, "Be quiet. Don't make any noise. If you do, I'll kill you."

He and the other man in front got out and closed their doors almost without sound. Then the man next to me got out, while the others opened my door and slipped a plastic bag over my head. The driver said in a whisper, "Get out but don't make any noise." He grasped me firmly by the arm. I started to reach for my shoes but they were gone. The driver said in a low voice, "What's the matter? Get out!" So I got out in my stocking feet.

Once out of the car, one of the other men took my left arm in a firm grip. The driver pulled the plastic bag tight around my face and neck. The plastic sealed my mouth and nostrils each time I breathed in. In near panic, I whispered, "I can't breathe! Give me air!" And I tried to keep the plastic away with my free right hand.

All this happened as I was being forcibly walked across a cement floor, tripping on small objects as I went. We seemed to be in some kind of a large building, like a garage or warehouse. I could not hear anyone making sounds, but from their whispering I guessed that other people were not far away.

We walked a short distance, then through what seemed to be a doorway into a room. Someone else was there, another man. From behind, he removed the plastic bag, very carefully replacing it with a cloth blindfold tied around my head. Then he said, "Lie down! Face down!"

I found myself lying on a bed. He spread my hands and feet. There seemed to be someone else in the room. I also got the impression that the men who had grabbed me were no longer present. Yet I could hear just the suggestion of a brief conversation in whispers.

After a minute or two the man who had blindfolded me began to search my pockets, one by one. From my pants pockets he took my money, my pocketknife, and my comb. After a minute, he returned my key case to my pocket. He felt his way through my jacket but didn't try to remove my glasses, for which I breathed a silent prayer of thanks. He tried to pull off my wedding ring, but it was tight and after several tugs he gave up. Thank God this symbol of my covenant with Carol would remain with me.

Several minutes passed in silence. Then this man said, "Passport?"

"No passport," I replied. "I don't have my passport with me. Passport at home."

Just yesterday I had put my passport away in a small strongbox in our bedroom, because we now had the new residence permits. Again I was happy that Carol had these documents.

"No passport," I repeated. "I'm an American."

More silence. I continued to wonder what would happen to me. Frank Regier, an engineering professor at the American University of Beirut, had been captured early that year and then released by Lebanese gendarmes, so the newspapers reported, after several months. Pictures taken upon his release showed Frank looking thin, shaggy, and tired. Would this kind of transformation happen to me?

I recalled the story of David Dodge, longtime resident of Lebanon and acting president of the American University. He had been abducted and held for a year. I knew nothing about his condition or how he had been released, but a year was a long time. What could I expect?

Emil Aghabi came to mind; he had disappeared along with a young man riding in the same taxi. I knew Emil well; he was a director of the Joint Christian Committee for service to Palestinian refugees in Lebanon, an arm of the Middle East Council of Churches. I had often asked about him, as had many others, but there was no trace of him. Was he dead or alive? No one knew. I realized that I might be joining the untold number of men who had vanished over the preceding nine years.

My memory conjured up stories of other persons, some of them held for ransom. I remembered the many conversations I had had during my ministry, with relatives who were trying to locate and negotiate the release of their loved ones. I had looked into the eyes of Lebanese friends faced with uncertainty and tragedy, trying to discover a ray of hope as we talked in a hallway, or in the corner of a staircase, or on the sidewalk. Again and again came the phrases: "Life is cheap. When someone is taken or killed, no one will pay attention. It is as if no one will ask about him. He is gone!"

Some captives were later freed, but many had indeed died, and later their bodies were found, too often mutilated. It was not a very cheery thought as I lay spread-eagled before my captives. *Lord, you know what I am. You know what is going on. Help me to trust you.*

Another man was at my side. "Who are you?"

"I am Benjamin Weir, an American. I am a pastor."

"What church?"

"The National Evangelical Synod of Syria and Lebanon."

"You work with Lebanese churches?"

"No, I'm a pastor. A Protestant pastor. Protestant. *Injili.*"

"You Maronite?"

"No. Not American University, Near East School of Theology. Teach of God."

English was not getting us very far, but I stuck to it, though I was greatly tempted to clarify my status in Arabic. However, I reasoned as I had done in other ambiguous or dangerous situations: It is best to assume the role of ignorant foreigner. I didn't trust the men who had taken me, nor the ones to whom they seemed to have delivered me. I had no idea what they wanted—ransom, money, my life, information, a public mock trial, or something else. So I would be reserved, not offering information about myself, lie low, and wait to see what they would conclude for themselves.

I also hoped that if they regarded me as an uninformed foreigner, of no value to them, they would let me go. I must be very careful not to speak Arabic, for to do so would arouse their suspicions. However, I could understand what they said to one another, and that would give me clues as to their purpose.

I was marshaling my resources for whatever terrors might lie ahead.

2

"What is your name?
Your maiden name?
Your husband's name?
His mother's maiden name?"

Tuesday, May 8, 1984, is a date Ben and I will never forget, although we remember the details of the actual kidnapping somewhat differently. We were headed out our gate to the street, moving at a good clip because we both were due at the Near East School of Theology shortly. I was walking a bit ahead of Ben to skirt a telephone pole, intent on our destination.

Two young men simultaneously got out of a white car parked directly across the street. *Unusual* flashed through my mind. One went directly over to Ben, who was now a short distance behind me. I thought he said something like "Come with me." The other young man dashed to the building next to ours, looked around, and then returned to join the man who had approached Ben.

"Come with me."

"No, I don't want to go with you."

Ben drew back, fear beginning to show on his face. Only one thought filled my mind: Oh, God! It's happening, it's happening. They are kidnapping Ben!

I started to shout and scream, "Help! Help! They're kidnapping my husband!" I dashed back to where the men were grappling with Ben, who was resisting with all his strength. Wouldn't someone hear me? My throat was tight with fear. I couldn't shout loud enough. "Help! Help! Oh, God, help us!"

One of the men grabbed hold of Ben's tie in such a way as to choke him. He could hardly breathe. His face was flushed; his eyes bulged with fear and the knowledge that he couldn't resist these men much longer. The expression of helplessness and pain on his face would remain in my memory for many months.

One of the men gave Ben a hard blow on the side of his head that knocked him off his feet. He shoved Ben into the car and the two men jumped in also, one on each side of him. "Oh, God! What shall I do?"

I knew that I had to keep my presence of mind if I was going to help him. Auto plates. I tried to get the license plate number. No plates!

Assistance from someone else. I had to get help. There was no one on that short street except an old woman headed in the opposite direction. Wouldn't anyone hear my cries?

Perhaps I could somehow stop them. I dashed over to the car and opened the front door. Could I get in the front seat and try to delay them? I didn't see any guns. I hesitated. It was madness to consider getting in, but what could I do? The third young man, the driver of the car, reached over and slammed the front door of the car shut. I tried to remember his face: hard, determined, a mustache, no beard. The car sped away, with me running, shouting, and screaming after it.

Children gathering for school at the end of our street said there had been a backup car. Both cars would have had to pass in front of the police station at the intersection of our street and Bliss Street. I knew there would be police standing out in front of the station. Could I get help there? Because Lebanon was nine years into a chaotic civil war, services were badly disrupted. The police had not solved a major crime in years. Nonetheless, it was worth a try.

I ran into the police station shouting, "Help! They've kidnapped my husband! Please, go after the car, a white car!"

No response. The police, not fully understanding, just looked at me. I switched to Arabic.

I was steered into the office of the station chief. "Please help me. Go after the car!"

The chief of police tried to calm me. "Don't worry," he said. "We will have your husband back soon." I was ushered into another office.

"Please go after the car."

"Don't worry. We will alert our men at all the roadblocks. We will stop the getaway car."

I was greatly agitated. Nobody seemed in any hurry. There were forms to fill out: What is your name? Your maiden name? Your husband's name? His mother's maiden name? I was so restless. "Please let me go! I want to leave—to go to friends who can help me."

The chief of police continued calmly. "We will help you. What is your husband's occupation?"

"He is a Protestant pastor."

"What is that?"

I tried to explain. No one at the police station knew anything about the Protestant church. "A priest," someone offered. "No . . . yes, a priest," I finally agreed. "Like a priest." I paced the floor, frightened and agitated.

The form was finally filled out. I had already wasted too much time. "Please let me go," I begged.

"Don't worry, your husband will be with you tonight," they said.

I wanted to believe this optimistic promise, but because of the political chaos in the country, I knew that the police force had been rendered largely ineffective. Frightened now to be out on the street alone, I asked for someone to escort me to the seminary, a few blocks away. The officer cheerfully agreed, and away we went on foot.

The Near East School of Theology is a Protestant interdenominational seminary at the graduate school level. It provides academic preparation for young men and women who plan to serve the Protestant community in the Middle East in various capacities. I was on the faculty there, and I was on my way to class when Ben was taken.

I rushed into the seminary building and up to the boardroom, where the meeting Ben was supposed to be attending was taking place. I burst unceremoniously into the room. "Ben has been kidnapped!" There was a brief moment of stunned silence as the news sank in. Then, as I knew would happen, they burst into action, telephoning anyone they knew with influence who might be able to help and encouraging me, as an American citizen, to turn to my government for protection and aid. I telephoned the American Embassy. "My husband has been kidnapped."

"How do you know?"

"I was with him."

"Where are you? We'll send someone up immediately to talk to you."

I recounted the tale of Ben's capture to a young American, who listened carefully and asked a few questions for clarification. As someone who was assigned to be "out on the streets," he knew the militias and promised that he would try to get information.

This man is surely in danger himself, I thought. What keeps *him* from getting kidnapped? (Later that day I was told by Lebanese security that his name was indeed on a hit list. They also told me they had warned the American Embassy that there would be renewed efforts to kidnap Americans. They voiced the opinion that embassy personnel did not take them seriously. Why hadn't the embassy contacted our school? I fumed. Surely they could have warned us!)

The interview over, I decided to call the embassy for an appointment with the U.S. ambassador. I had had so little contact with the embassy that I didn't even know his name. In any case, it turned out that he was in Washington at that moment. Instead, I met with the Deputy Chief of Mission, who spoke to me in clipped tones.

"What do you expect?" he asked, after I had retold my tale. "Hasn't the embassy suggested that all nonessential Americans leave? We can't keep our own personnel safe from kidnapping."

"The kidnapping of Americans is a response to our foreign policy," I observed. His retort to my observation came stinging back. "You don't expect us to change our foreign policy, do you?" This discouraging exchange convinced me there was no help here. Embassy people were themselves under pressure and probably fearful for their own safety, I told myself. On April 18, 1983, just a year earlier, the U.S. Embassy itself, situated on a stretch of road along the Mediterranean Sea in West Beirut, had been destroyed. The early-afternoon bombing ripped through the seven-story structure and rocked the whole area. I heard it in my own office at the seminary several blocks away; the sound was deafening. The students rushed into my office with the news that the U.S. Embassy had been the target. The extensive power of the explosion brought fear to the faces of Americans and Arabs alike. This attack represented a huge escalation of resentment against Americans.

Sixty-three people, American and Lebanese, were killed, with more than a hundred injured. This was no ordinary car bomb. We learned that a car driven by a daring suicide driver had rammed the front wall, shattering the whole building in a powerful explosion. Then fire broke out and destroyed what was left. It was no wonder that embassy personnel were as anxious and testy as we were.

At the end of the interview, I was told to keep in touch; someone was assigned to the task of giving aid and comfort to the families of the kidnapped.

This kind of service was becoming increasingly necessary. Already this year Frank Regier, a professor of electrical engineering at the American University, had been kidnapped on February 10. Happily, he was freed two months later by Nabih Berri's Shiite militia. Jeremy Levin of Cable News Network had been kidnapped on March 7, and William Buckley, CIA station chief at the embassy, on March 18. And now Ben. . . .

Later I called on Dianne Dillard at the American Embassy, who expressed genuine sympathy and concern. She offered her veranda as a place to relax and helped me make phone calls and send mail to the United States. I was grateful that in the midst of the strain and stress of the chaos of Lebanon, she was able to communicate a sense of care and comfort. I learned later that she had received a special commendation for quick action in setting up an office for the Consular Section in her building following the car bombing of the U.S. Embassy a year before.

However, for the moment, I was totally absorbed by the shock and fear of Ben's capture. I had to inform my family. Ben was taken at around eight fifteen in the morning. California time was ten hours behind Lebanon time. I must reach them before they heard the news from the media. A colleague drove me from the seminary to her apartment building, where a friend graciously offered the use of her international phone line. After what seemed like forever, I was able to reach our daughter Susan. I woke her up at five in the morning.

"Sue, I'm afraid I have some bad news. Your father was kidnapped early this morning." Could this really be happening to us? I tearfully gave her the details.

"Oh, Mother, what can I do?"

I asked her to contact our other children and family members. Christine was in Saudi Arabia, Ann and John in California. I especially wanted my father, Albert Swain, who was concerned for our safety, to hear the news from us.

Of course she could tell the others, and she did. This was the beginning of many telephone calls and radio and TV appearances she was to make on behalf of her father. She became my contact with the rest of our family and faithfully telephoned me in Beirut each week to give me encouragement and moral support. Sue was the one who was constantly in touch with the Lebanon desk at the State Department for information and assistance. Sue, John, and Ann met that weekend to organize themselves into a team. (A telex from Chris the day after Ben's capture confirmed that she had received the news, would contact everyone she knew with possible influence, and was praying earnestly for me.)

I returned to the seminary to be with friends, students, and faculty. How really wonderful it is to be surrounded by caring people! I was close to tears.

I had avoided the press, not knowing how to deal with the media people who had descended on the seminary. The Rev. Dr. Salim Sahiouny, head of the Arabic-speaking Presbyterian church and responsible for American Presbyterians working in Lebanon, released a statement on my behalf. He noted that Ben had been working with the Presbyterian Church (U.S.A.) in church-related activities and with international nongovernmental organizations in emergency relief programs. He appealed to all parties and militia groups to help obtain Ben's release.

The seminary staff offered to have someone walk home with me. It was getting late, and I accepted the offer. As we approached the apartment house, television cameras were waiting to record my return to our home. I am not naturally a public person and I did not want to talk with these aggressive people, who seemed to sprout lights and lenses. Ben must have had his keys with him, so I had our apartment lock changed. Now I shut the door on the world outside. The rooms were lonely and empty without Ben. I was nervous, afraid to be in my apartment alone, exhausted by the day's events. Would the kidnappers come to the apartment to demand a ransom or to question me? In this frame of mind, I was grateful for the gracious invitation of my upstairs neighbors, Ralph and Laure Crow, to have dinner and stay the night with them.

A thousand thoughts went racing through my mind. Ralph usually left the apartment house before Ben in the morning. Were the captors after Ben or Ralph or just any American? Ralph was a professor at the American University of Beirut. Did the captors want to "replace" Frank Regier, who had been released earlier? (Frank told me later that his captors had said to him that their directions were to kidnap an American from the American University.) What were the demands for Ben's release, or had he already been killed as others had been?

I sank into the Crows' guest bed that night in exhaustion and fear. The tears flooded down my cheeks as I prayed.

> O God, where is Ben? Keep him safe. Help him to be aware of your presence. Help us to know what to do. Don't let me lose sight of your love for us. O God, help us.

We had no electricity in our sector of West Beirut that night because of the shelling and destruction of the power plant, so I had gone to bed by candlelight. The strange bed didn't seem right. I missed Ben's comfort and strength. The full weight of what had happened that day descended upon me. I suddenly felt so very alone.

As I tossed and turned, I could hear reports of Ben's kidnapping on the BBC and the Voice of America broadcasts from the small transistor radio next to my pillow. Oh, God, could this really be happening to us?

May 8, 1984. A day I'll never forget.

3

"Count your many blessings, name them one by one."

Riding in my mummy case, my mind came back to the present crisis. The smells from the exhaust had blown away. *Lord, keep me from being overcome with panic. I have fresh air, and I am still breathing.*

Recounting to myself each step in my entombment made me relax and feel a bit better about the situation. I had been calm under stress, and my captors had not been especially cruel. I tried to concentrate on what lay ahead.

The truck lurched forward, its gears grinding and its joints creaking as we bounced over a rough road. There were ups and downs, turns and counterturns. I quickly lost all sense of direction. Where were we going? Sometimes we were on hard surfaces while at other times we were jolted from one rut to another. Whenever we hit a shell hole in the road, my back slammed down against the hard bottom of the box, and on the bumps I did what I could to keep my nose from smashing into the metal top a few inches from my face.

How long the trip was I could not measure in time. Though it seemed like an eternity, it was probably not much more than an hour and a half. On the fairly smooth stretches, or at brief stops I supposed were checkpoints, I tried to remember scripture or hymns. Bits and pieces flashed into my mind:

My grace is sufficient for you.
God will not permit us to be put to a trial beyond our capacity to bear.
Amazing grace—how sweet the sound—that saved a wretch like me!

As the journey proceeded and I had no idea when or where it might end, I thanked God over and over again, who up to that moment had sustained and kept me. How long could I stand being a mummy in a box? My body would be bruised and aching tomorrow. But I had no choice.

After a time the driver stopped the truck, left the cab, and went away. When he returned, he started the motor, ground the gears again, and we traveled for a few more minutes. Then we drove into a building; I could hear the echo of the truck's engine. The motor stopped, the driver got out, and a large metal door dropped into place.

Someone came around back to my box, opened the lid, and pulled me out by the shoulders. Then he grasped me around the chest and stood me upright on the floor. This guy must really be strong, I thought.

How good it was to be out of that box and back on terra firma! I didn't feel very steady on my feet. The man was holding on to me and he must have sensed my unsteadiness, because he lifted me a few feet and leaned me against a wall. I was surrounded by voices. Several men seemed to be inspecting me. They had been awaiting my arrival.

Someone began cutting the tape on my ankles and legs and pulling it off in pieces. Next my hands and lower arms were freed. I began flexing hands and arms and legs. I was stiff and sore all over, but very glad to be alive.

Suddenly a man put his back against mine, clenched his arms around my waist, hefted me onto his back, and carried me upstairs, where several voices were speaking Lebanese colloquial Arabic. More of the tape binding my chest, shoulders, and neck was removed. Someone said to me, "Sit." I sat, expecting to find a chair under me, but instead I dropped down to a mattress on the floor. My chest and neck were sore from the tight bonds, and I could not close my jaw all the way.

As I sat there, someone moved next to me and said in English, "Quiet! No speak!" Then he took my left hand and began pulling on my tight wedding ring. He kept pulling and turning it. The pain was so acute I worried that he would dislocate my finger or cut it off with a knife to get the ring. He finally succeeded in pulling it off. He went through all my pockets, found a few coins in my small money pocket, and took those too.

Inside my wedding ring, symbol of togetherness for thirty-five years, were inscribed the words *More than conquerors* and a verse that added, *through Him who loved us.* The ring might go, but the sense of the common calling shared by Carol and me would remain.

After a while the remaining tape on my eyes and head was cut loose and pulled off without ceremony or hesitation—a bit of my hair went with it. While the tape was being removed, a cloth bandage was tied over my eyes. My jacket was stripped off and taken away. A man

said, "Stand." He led me by the arm down the hallway to the bathroom and stood guard behind me, saying, "Look to the wall and see
the toilet, but don't turn!"

When finished, I tied the blindfold back in place, felt along the wall
to the basin, and washed my hands. Without thinking, I drank copi-
ously to quench my thirst and wiped my hands on my shirt.

Then I was led into another room. Again I was told to sit. This time
I let myself down carefully onto a mattress; it was on the floor. He
said, "Move back." I did so until my back was against a wall. Then
he told me to stretch out my left arm. I obeyed, and he wrapped the
end of a chain around my wrist and closed it snugly with a padlock.
He said sternly, "You not see," and touched the strip of cloth covering my eyes. I understood that I must remain blindfolded. "Sh-sh-sh
. . . no sound. You quiet. You much quiet." He went out, sliding a door
closed behind him. I heard him lock it. I was alone.

I sat there for a while with my eyes covered, wondering where I
was. The guard did not return and there was no sound of footsteps.
I figured that the noise of unlocking and opening the sliding door
would warn me of his return. Carefully, I raised the cloth strip
enough so I could see.

I was in a bare room, its walls and woodwork painted a light gray.
The floor was covered with the ceramic tile squares so often found
in the city's buildings, with louvered shutters closing off glass French
doors.

I was sitting on a foam rubber mattress a few inches thick, six feet
long, about three and a half feet wide. It had seen better days and
showed sunken spots in the middle. The pattern on the cover was
stained, and the underside was full of dust and dirt. On the mattress
was an uncovered pillow of equal vintage.

I examined the link chain. It was stamped HARDENED STEEL. The
padlock likewise looked sturdy, hardened, and bore the usual announcement, MADE IN CHINA. There was no chance of undoing that
restraint. I counted thirty-three inch-sized links between my wrist
and the radiator, to which the chain was fastened with another padlock.

I was still examining my surroundings when I heard footsteps outside my door. I pulled the cloth strip over my eyes and sat cross-
legged on my mattress with head slightly bowed. The guard came in
saying, "Sanweesh. Good." He put in my hands two sandwiches
wrapped in paper and left. A few minutes later he reappeared and
gave me a bottle. After he was gone, I saw that I had an orange
carbonated beverage and two chicken sandwiches rolled in Arabic
bread.

I was hungry and they tasted good. I judged that it was probably early afternoon. I began reviewing the events of the day, returning again and again to the scene of my capture. How could I have avoided it? There was no satisfactory answer. Had the three men in the car been lying in wait for me to appear? It happened so quickly I knew they must have been prepared, but did they want me or someone else? Was Carol all right? I fervently prayed that she be kept safe and that she have the wisdom to leave Lebanon immediately, but that too was out of my hands. I must entrust her to the care of a loving Father, as I did myself. I tried to size up my own situation as best I could: I am a captive. I see no way to escape. I have my clothes, but everything else has been taken. I can understand my captors, but they have difficulty communicating with me in English. Maybe I will find an opportunity to teach them some English; that would be meaningful work. I have one important resource they cannot touch, faith in the living God. This foundation can make all the difference for me.

One thing I know and that is the date. Today is Tuesday, May 8, 1984. I must remember that in order to keep track of time. I need a calendar, so that I can count the days. When I'm released I want to tell what happened to me in sequence. I don't want to lose my basic orientation. I need a time frame, but I don't have any way to keep a written record.

As I struggled with this question, I noticed small holes in the wall facing me, perhaps fifteen feet away. Some previous occupant must have hung pictures there. As I began counting those pockmarks, I realized they were fixed points on which I could hang my mental calendar. I started with the eighth and included marks on the other walls until I had counted out the remaining days in May. This method of counting would help me remember our daughter Susan, whose birthday was May 10, and the Memorial Day holiday.

I felt a mood of challenge rising within me. These men had seized me and thought of themselves as victors, but I would not accept being a victim, even though I might appear submissive and unknowing.

I didn't trust these men. I believed them to be dangerous and unpredictable. I resented their strong-arm tactics, their kidnapping me for their own purposes, whatever those purposes were. I hated their denying me my freedom and preventing me from continuing what I saw as good and worthwhile service. They cut me off from my wife, family, friends, colleagues, and students. It was unjust and wrong, and I would resist as best I could without openly inviting further violence. In a small counseling group three years earlier, an angry colleague had described me as unable to explode with anger but being passively aggressive. I would live up to this reputation for passive aggression. I would use that tactic for my own survival. As I reflected on my mood of resistance and my newly created calendar, I also experienced a sense of life and inner strength. What a gift of God! I thanked him for it. I didn't want to slip into a slough of despond, a quagmire of self-pity. *Lord, help me to discover the resources you provide and to use them creatively for my survival and for your glory.*

Suddenly there was a noise at the door. Again I pulled my cloth strip into place and sat passively. The guard entered and said, "Hot. House hot." I heard him open the French doors, and a brisk breeze began to blow through the room. I heard him open the shutters to the outside and stand in the wind, but I didn't dare look. The breeze was cool and I began to feel chilly, even to shiver a bit in my shirt sleeves. He must have noticed because he asked, "You cold?"

"Yes, I'm cold."

He closed the shutters and the doors. He went and got a blanket, which he dropped on the bed. Then he went out, locking the door behind him. This simple act of care was further confirmation that the guard wanted me to keep well and alive. I arranged the pillow, stretched out, and relaxed. Thankful for life, rest, and a blanket, I soon dropped off to sleep.

I awoke refreshed by my nap. What other gifts would God show me in addition to sleep, a blanket, a calendar, and a spirit of resistance and survival? Once again I lifted my blindfold and began examining the room. What was there here that could bring me close to the sustaining presence of God? I let my imagination have total freedom to see what might come to mind.

Looking up, I examined an electric wire hanging from the ceiling. The bulb and socket had been removed, so that it ended in an arc with three wires exposed. To me, those wires seemed like three fingers. I could see a hand and an arm reaching downward—like the Sistine Chapel in Rome, Michelangelo's fresco of God reaching out his hand and finger toward Adam, creating the first living human being. Here God was reaching toward me, reminding me, saying, "You're alive. You are mine; I've made you and called you into being for a divine purpose." This insight startled me. It was a bolt of inspiration out of heaven.

What else? I began counting the horizontal slats of the shutters outside the French doors. There were 120. What could those horizontal pieces of wood stand for, so many of them? That's it! Many of them, a crowd! A cloud of witnesses past and present, who through crises and times of trial have observed and perceived the faithfulness of God Recognizing that I am surrounded by such a great cloud of witnesses, let me lay aside every weight and sin and run with patience the race set before me, looking to Jesus, the initiator and completer of our faith. He endured the cross with its shame and is now seated at the right hand of God on my behalf.

This recital of the basics of my faith sent a chill through me. What a message! That's the guide I need. I desperately need patience in my present setting.

My thinking was being led by the classic statements of the Christian faith. There seemed to be a flow from these doctrinal streams of expression into my own situation.

Then my eyes lighted on two white circles near the ceiling, one on the right-hand wall, the other on the left. Everybody in Lebanon knows what they are, plastic covers for electrical connections. Yet what can they be for me? What comes in a pair? Ears! They are the ears of God. The Lord hears the groaning of the saints. God promised Moses guidance and support and issued him a calling in the wilderness at the burning bush.

The Protestant Reformers, and especially John Calvin, received the same assurance in times of stress. I remembered that Calvin had emblazoned on his seal the burning bush that Moses saw, adding his response: "My heart I give thee, Lord, promptly and sincerely." *So listen to me, dear God, I also surrender to your care and will. Give me the promise of the burning bush.*

My eyes returned to the electric wire, following it up toward the ceiling. There I noticed a commonplace item for the first time. A hook of reinforcing rod had been bent out of the concrete form before pouring, forming almost a closed ellipse. Every home and apartment had one near the ceiling on which to hang a light, so the electric wire would not have to bear the weight of the fixture. What could that elevated ellipse be for me? An eye! The eye of God— admittedly anthropomorphic, but a reminder that in his sovereignty and wisdom his ways are not thwarted but ongoing.

As a boy in junior high school art class I had found it difficult to visualize forms and reproduce them, but now I found my imagination coming alive. What else did I see? On a shelf in one corner of the room stood a game bird, perhaps shot and stuffed by a former occupant. A gray bird, like a dove. A dove! That's it, Noah's bird, the one released from the window of the ark. It went searching and brought back a bit of greenery, a sign of life, a new beginning, hope in the chaos.

Later, the Spirit as a dove alighted on Jesus as he arose from the waters of baptism to fulfill his calling in public ministry. Here, too, was a call for me to walk with him in Galilee and on the road to

Jerusalem. The dove would direct my attention and assist my spirit in some new way to "hear the beloved Son."

Sounds around me aroused images that were more ambiguous and troublesome. I listened to footsteps outside my door and speculated, without profit, on their comings and goings. I heard Arabic voices but could not make out what they were saying. Occasionally I would hear the motor of a vehicle passing by outside but could conclude nothing. I noticed the voices of children, but they disappeared in the distance. As each sound approached the building, I hoped someone was coming to rescue me, even though my reason told me that was not probable. *How long, O Lord, will this go on?* There was no answer.

As the light coming through the slats of the shutter faded, I began to get settled mentally for the night. Again I reviewed the events of the day. I was here, alone but alive. I had better make the best of it and adjust. I still had things to appreciate. My body, though sore, was still whole. I had survived capture and a terrifying ride. My captors seemed to want me alive rather than dead. I was sure of Carol's love and deep concern. I had happy recollections of our family, and most recently of our daughter Chris, who had visited us from Saudi Arabia less than two months ago.

Out of past memories came the phrase, "Count your many blessings, name them one by one." This statement seemed appropriate. I fingered the links of the chain that bound me. Then, beginning at my ankle, I began counting: health, life, food, mattress, pillow, blanket, Carol, Chris, John, Sue, Ann, faith, hope, prayer, Jesus, Holy Spirit, Father's love. . . . I reached the thirty-third link before I was finished, so I returned in my counting from the radiator toward my ankle. This chain will be my Protestant rosary, reminding me of God's gifts.

Before it was completely dark, a guard came again. He said, "Face the wall." I did. "Now take your blindfold off and put this on." He handed me something solid that had a strap on it. I took off the cloth slowly. I found I was holding plastic ski goggles in which the eye holes had been taped over with thick plastic adhesive tape. I put it on my head and the guard checked to see that the headband was tight. He said, "You keep this on. Good. No see." Then he went out. I lifted the mask to my forehead and decided it was a good exchange. It would be ready so that at a moment's notice I could pull it down over my eyes. I thanked God for this new convenience.

I could now imagine that the sun had set. In the twilight there came to mind the hymn, "Abide with me: fast falls the eventide." I felt vulnerable, helpless, lonely, and that brought tears to my eyes. But then I remembered the promise of Jesus, "If you abide in me and

my words abide in you, ask what you will and it shall be done unto
you."

> Lord, I remember your promise, and I think it applies to me too.
> I've done nothing to deserve it but receive it as a free gift. I'm in
> need. I need you. I need your assurance and guidance to be faithful
> to you in this situation. Help me to live trustingly with you in an
> intimate relationship. Teach me what I need to learn. Deliver me
> from this place and this captivity if it is your will. If it is not your
> will to set me free, help me to accept whatever is involved. Show
> me your gifts and enable me to recognize them as coming from you.
> Thank you for your encouraging presence. Praise be to you.

There came to mind automatically the evening song we had often
sung together at the close of the day with Beirut students in retreats.
I hummed it softly so the guards wouldn't hear me. "All praise to
thee, my God, this night. . . ." The tears now were prompted by
gratitude and a sense of companionship and intimacy.

As darkness became complete, I found myself recalling one hymn
after another. Of some I could remember several verses, and where
there was a gap I could improvise. Of others, I could only remember
a phrase or two. I was surprised to see how many came to mind.

It was time to get settled for the night. As I was preparing to
stretch out and find a comfortable position for my aching neck, chest,
and legs, I heard footfalls near my door. Quickly, I pulled on the ski
mask and sat up. The door slid back. The guard came in and said,
"Food." I put out my hands and he gave me a sandwich. "Tea." He
poured me a glass of tea. Then he went out. Once the door closed,
I found I had a generous apricot jam sandwich rolled in a large loaf
of Arabic bread and a hot glass of sweetened tea. I was hungry and
it tasted good. I ate slowly. Another gift.

Once again I stretched out, pulled the blanket over me, and
dropped off to sleep, thinking how much I wished Carol were near.

4

"He is my friend. . . .
I want to know if he is being held
in this part of the city."

I returned to the seminary early the next morning, after a restless night in our neighbors' apartment. Safely at my desk, I sat for a while before going to class and reviewed my situation. I felt a deep loneliness. I hoped Ben would be freed soon. But there were still six weeks left of the school semester. I was teaching a course at the American University as well as my usual seminary courses. Didn't I have a commitment to my students to complete the term's work? My teaching load would also give shape to my life and help me maintain a sense of direction during the days ahead. And I could spend all my spare time working for Ben's release.

Yet how should I even begin the task of recovering Ben from unknown kidnappers? Three other Americans had been taken in similar circumstances over the past few months. Who was behind these dreadful events?

As I sat at my desk, I read of Ben's capture in the *Daily Star,* an English-language newspaper published in Beirut. The article suggested a connection between the kidnapping of Americans and a recent announcement that three men in Kuwait, convicted of involvement in the December 1983 bombing of the French and American embassies there, would be executed "soon." If the three in Kuwait were killed, would the Americans be killed? Had Ben been captured as a bargaining chip in a deadly political game?

The May 10 edition of that same paper stated that an unidentified man had telephoned the Beirut offices of Agence France Presse, the French news agency, and read a statement in Arabic that said, "The Islamic Jihad organization claims it is responsible for the abduction of the American minister." The caller had said that the kidnapping was undertaken in answer to President Reagan's challenge that they could not drive every American from their soil. What was the truth?

Sometime later, a Shiite woman friend knocked on the door of my office. We embraced each other. Our friendship dated back to Ben and my early days in the market town of Nabatiyeh, where we spent our first five years in Lebanon. A teacher, she now lived in the southern part of the city of Beirut, where the majority were of the Shiite community. There were tears in her eyes and in mine as she talked of her sadness over Ben's kidnapping. She told me that the day he was taken she was carrying a letter of his in her purse, an introduction to officials at the American University of Beirut, where she was hoping to enroll her daughter in a public health program.

As we sat and talked, she described her concern for Ben and said she wanted to help. If Ben had been taken by one of the radicalized Shiite groups, perhaps he would be held in her neighborhood. She would try to find out if he was there.

Some days later she returned. She told me that she had gotten permission from her husband before venturing out. She had changed from schoolteacher garb to simple dress, put a scarf over her head, and made the rounds of shops, butchers, grocers, and vendors of all kinds of wares in the southern suburbs of Beirut. She asked them if an American might be hidden somewhere in the area. Some had angrily inquired why she was making this effort. "He is my friend and a good man," she replied. "He has helped me many times. I want to know if he is being held in this part of the city." The answer she got was always the same. "He is not here."

I felt the tears come to my eyes as she related her story. What a faithful and courageous friend! She had put her own life at risk to help us.

She told me how a year before she had been in her kitchen when a sniper's bullet zinged through the window. Her left arm was hit and a large chunk of flesh torn away. She was laid up for six months and unable to teach school. Her house in this Shiite community faced east toward the Christian sector of town. She knew that there were snipers active that day. She had tried to be careful, but she needed something from the kitchen.

In her neighborhood at that time the situation was so tense it was not safe to leave the house. The stores could not be resupplied. It was difficult to get the simplest medicine, even aspirin. There was extensive destruction of apartments and other buildings. Electrical service was intermittent. Telephones were out. The roads were pitted by repeated shellings. It was hard, she said, to live under those circumstances. But where could she and her family go?

She said she was deeply saddened by the warfare. Why did it continue? Arabs and Israeli could get together. They could all begin over and get a fresh start. Doesn't God intend us to live together in peace?

I remembered other friends from our stay in the town of Nabatiyeh: the doctor who lived nearby and treated Ben when he had jaundice, and his daughter who taught us Arabic. She told us many jokes and folk stories to entertain us as we learned the new language. Her mother and her visiting friends patiently listened to these stories as I haltingly repeated them for practice. We learned to share in the life of the village and developed an appreciation of Shiite religious festivals. We learned of the faithful women who discipline themselves with prayer and fasting. What a unique experience we had had, developing good friends among people of a different language, culture, and religion. We treasured this orientation to life in Lebanon.

I also remembered the time that Imm Ziad, a Palestinian mother of eight children, came to Ben's office. Her family had lost all their personal belongings during terrible shelling in the southern suburbs of Beirut and had had to flee their cement-block home in the refugee camp. One of her children was mentally retarded. Ben found her a job, got the children back into school after a two-year absence, and helped an older daughter enroll in a secretarial course.

Ben actually saved this family, as part of his life and ministry. Because of his faith, Ben naturally cared for people. He was not an ugly American who came to push others into the narrow confines of his own Western culture.

Ben's love of Christ was expressed through a love which touched and enriched the lives of those around us. Yet this is no reason why we should be spared from the sufferings experienced by everyone else in Lebanon. When Ben was kidnapped, I learned that the life of faith does not protect us from situations where we feel helplessness, loneliness, and the pain of suffering.

5

*"We know you work with the American
Embassy. . . . We know you go there."*

I awoke from a sound sleep as light began filtering in through the shutters. The distant barking of a dog drifted across my consciousness. After a while a rooster crowed. Then a truck rattled along the street, and a motorcycle snarled past. I could hear the voices of two men close by. Could these sounds tell me anything about where I was? The cockcrow did not necessarily mean I was in the country. Our West Beirut neighbors had kept a few chickens on the rooftops of their apartment houses.

At least I knew what day it was—the next day. So I sat up, looked at my calendar, and fixed Wednesday, May ninth, on the second nail hole. Keeping track of time was vital. If I lost my orientation to life in the world, I could become lost as a person.

I heard a few birds chirping nearby. There must be trees near the building, like our apartment in West Beirut, I thought. What a lively and joyful sound! Carol and I used to enjoy sitting on the veranda of our apartment, overlooking the tree-shaded garden, listening to the birds. I felt a serenity just recalling our quiet times together. How marvelous it is to share the pleasure of a special person's companionship! Gray walls, a locked and guarded door, and a length of chain could in no way cut me off from the boundless stream of life. It was a tremendous realization at this moment of my captivity.

It was not enough just to reflect about my part in God's plan, I must be active. I need to structure time. It is my responsibility to preserve my health and be ready for whatever comes. I decided to exercise in spite of the chain and in some sense overcome its constraints.

I sat up—and felt every disgruntled muscle. At least I could close my jaw now, tender though it was. My head turned, but my neck objected by sending sharp pains. Arms worked, but pectoral muscles were not ready for pushups. Legs creaked, but I could stand on them in a kind of hunched posture.

I began with sit-ups, then bicycling on my back, a few back arches, then body twists, squatting exercises, bending from the waist, and arm stretches to the limit of my chain. To exercise felt good, except for sore muscles. I examined my arms, my torso, and my legs. I was thankful for a body that still functioned and for life itself—after yesterday's ride.

Yet, what can I do about time? I was to be a steward of that, too, and had plenty of it. "To whom much is given, of him shall much be required." Here was a resource to be put to use. Using "all the time in the world" would require creativity and structure.

My physical mobility is limited. I am like a dog on a leash. However, I am not a dog, I am a man created in the image of God and redeemed by Jesus Christ, with a capacity for spiritual and intellectual potential.

I thought about my recent seven-month furlough in the United States and the decision Carol and I faced about whether to return to Lebanon. The Presbyterian Church's Program Agency people in New York had made it clear that we were not obligated to go back. In fact, I suspect they would have been relieved if we chose to go elsewhere. It was left up to us, in consultation with the Lebanese church body under whom we worked.

Our family and friends didn't want us to go back. New violence and heavy fighting had again erupted in the nine-year civil war. First one person and then another showed me fresh pictures and news reports. The worst was the ugly assassination of Malcolm Kerr, the president of the American University of Beirut, on January 18, 1984, in the hallway outside his office. Was it right for us to return?

On the other hand, was it right not to return? We hoped for an end to the warfare and a chance to prepare Protestant leadership for the future. To do that we needed to be on the scene. Furthermore, we had a clear call from the Lebanese church to serve with them. During this period of agony and turmoil, they were asking us to demonstrate by our presence the solidarity of our Presbyterian Church with them, with the other churches, and with the suffering people of Lebanon.

As I had pondered this dilemma in private, I happened upon a saying of Christ in the New English Bible translation that made the edge even sharper. In Luke 9:24, I read and reread the words I could not avoid, "Whoever cares for his own safety is lost; but if a man will let himself be lost for my sake, that man is safe."

I had no desire to be a martyr. Yet I knew physical security could not be the most important criterion for our decision. In the face of uncertainty and threat (the situation to which Jesus spoke), the paramount consideration was faithfulness to Jesus and his cause. He offered no physical protection to his disciples then or now. But by facing the risks of serving others, they were to experience and live out the Father's self-giving love in the same way that Jesus was doing. To do so was profoundly worthwhile and resulted in a deeper kind of security than mere physical safety. I knew then that God's will was for Carol and me to proceed toward Lebanon.

I now sat as a prisoner of unknown forces. The golden opportunity to seek a life of spiritual growth was before me, yet I felt like a novice. It was true that I had made my commitment to Christ and accepted the new life he offered years ago. From that time on I had found meaning, joy, and direction in periods of daily Bible reading and prayer—sometimes longer, sometimes shorter, and sometimes not at all. For me the day was best when I began it with a sense of spiritual direction, commitment, and praise. Launching the day in this way gave me a vantage point at the beginning and a series of way stations throughout the day.

However, now the situation was different. There were no time constraints. Neither did I have the usual resources: Bible, devotional booklet, pad of paper and pencil, hymnbook, or other printed resources. This time I was really on my own.

I began with what I had: memory. A passage out of the past popped into mind. I couldn't remember where it occurred (later I found it in Proverbs 3:5). I let myself focus on basic aspects of the passage. My mind and spirit played with the message as I sat chained to a radiator in my room that second day.

> Trust in the LORD with all your heart,
> and do not rely on your own insight.
> In all your ways acknowledge him,
> and he will make straight your paths.

Trust. In the early days of my captivity I said repeatedly, *Lord, here I am. You know where I am, even if I do not. You know how I came here and what's going to happen. You know who my captors are, even if I do not. I'm helpless. I'm in your hands. Help me to trust you.*

I think of a struggling, suffering, stranded Palestinian family *(Lord, help them!).* I think also of a dozen students from South Sudan who have no scholarships, no work, no certainty they can stay in Lebanon, no assurance that they will have enough food *(God, be their sustenance!).* The people of voluntary international agencies will meet next Tuesday without me as chairperson *(Dear God, strengthen them in this time of need!).*

I also think of faithful colleagues and students at the seminary as they search for a new president and direction at this critical time *(God, sustain them!).* I particularly focus on my life with Carol as she faces the frustration, fear, and danger *(O God, keep her!).*

Yes, Lord, I've been busy these years, and in spite of the problems, uncertainties, and dangers I have been glad to be active in serving others. I confess that my service has never been perfect, never been complete. You know that in spite of my shortcomings I've regarded it as a way of serving you, and cooperating with your ongoing purpose in the world. Yet I also have the feeling and hope—yes, the conviction—that my activity and service with and for others is worthwhile in your eyes.

Lord, the truth is that I don't have any insight into what's happening to me. Of course, I know there are many armed groups out to kidnap people in Lebanon, and this radical militia is one of them. I feel sure I'm here because I'm an American, and experiencing anger toward Americans is not new to me. But what else?

They are telling me that I have been taken for "political reasons." What does that mean? Perhaps they think I'm linked with the CIA. Did the man who talked with me consider political reasons in taking me? Will such an assumption lead to interrogation and maybe torture? I don't have political connections. I know that and so do you. So the truth is my only defense.

I must remember not "to rely on my own insight" because I don't have any. I can easily imagine a wide range of possibilities: rescue, escape, execution, illness, dying, being injured by others in an attempt to storm this place. Or I might just wait, and wait, and wait until someday I'm set free, either sane or mad.

Lord, keep me from the fears of my own imaginings. Make my path to you unencumbered and direct.

As I prayed, God gave me the strength I needed. I began to sing, joyously but quietly, "Praise, my soul, the King of heaven." The words fit my mood and situation exactly. They were a sign to me of God's presence. I began reciting other scripture passages that came tumbling into my head. My mind turned to missionary colleagues in need of that same assurance, and I prayed for them by name—and of course I prayed for Carol.

I thought of other Americans in Beirut who might be in danger and prayed for them also. I remembered Christian friends on the seminary faculty, pastors, lay people, social workers, and students. My prayer also reached and embraced friends who were Shiite Muslims, Sunni Muslims, Druze, Kurds, Palestinians, Armenian Gregorians, Catholics, Greek Orthodox, and others.

My meditation was interrupted by footsteps and a noise at the door. Quickly, I donned my headgear. The door was pushed open along its groove. The guard greeted me. "Morning."

"Good morning," I answered.

"How are you?"

"Okay."

"Food."

He placed a sandwich into my outstretched hands. He also poured a glass of tea and went out. The sandwich proved to be another generous Arabic loaf with pieces of tuna and boiled eggs rolled inside. A very substantial breakfast, I thought with gratitude.

Sometime later the guard returned to take me to the bathroom. He unlocked the chain on my wrist. I walked in front of him, blindfolded but guided by his hand, down the hallway to the bathroom and felt my way to the toilet. There was no seat, but to my surprise there was a bit of toilet paper. I felt my way to the basin, turned on the faucet, found a bit of soap, and washed.

"Quick," the guard said impatiently.

"Is this tap water good for drinking?" I asked. I didn't want to take another chance on the water. In Lebanon almost all houses and apartments have separate systems for drinking and for washing. Water for cleaning tasks and bathing is usually stored in a cistern on the roof, where it tends to pick up dust or contamination. The guard replied that it was drinking water, so I cupped my hands, gulped some water, and dried my hands on my shirt. Then I walked as a blind man back to my room, to sit and be chained and left alone. At least this brief excursion was a change.

Around midday, there were more footsteps, the pushing back of the door, and the sounds of someone entering. This time a different voice said, "How are you?"

"Okay, thanks."

"What's your name?"

"Benjamin Weir. I'm a pastor."

"What pastor?"

"Pastor is a minister, serving a church. I'm a Protestant—*Injili.*"

"What church?"

"Protestant church. Lebanese church. National Evangelical Synod of Syria and Lebanon."

"You Catholic?"

"No, Protestant. A pastor. I also teach."

"What you teach?"

"I teach at the Near East School of Theology sometimes."

"What theology?"

"Theology is studying about God."

"Oh, you priest?"

"Well, not exactly, but like a priest. I'm a pastor."

"Okay. You American?"

"Yes, I'm an American."

Now a second voice, breath heavily scented by tobacco: "We know you work with the American Embassy."

"No, that's not true. I have nothing to do with the American Embassy."

"But we know you go there."

"Yes, I go to get my passport renewed when necessary, but I don't work with the embassy."

"Who do you know at the embassy?"

"Well, I know the Lebanese man in the consular section who renewed my passport."

"Who else do you know?"

"I don't know anyone else. I'm not even sure who the ambassador is now."

"We know you work with the embassy."

"You are wrong. I have no political connections."

"Maybe you don't work *at* the embassy, but we know you are a spiritual adviser."

"My friend, that's not true. You don't know much about the U.S. government if you think they have spiritual advisers. I'm not connected with the embassy in any way."

"We will give you time to think about the people you know at the embassy. I'll be back to get the names from you."

"I don't need time, because I don't know anyone there. I'm telling you the truth."

"We will be back later. For sure you know names."

With that parting remark the two men went out, leaving me in a quandary. How could I answer what I didn't know?

I was telling the truth. Did they intend to fabricate some story to frame me? Was this only the beginning of more severe questioning? Perhaps they wanted me to become increasingly anxious as they tightened the screws and then tried to extract information about other Americans I knew.

I thought of my missionary colleagues and the anxiety they must already be feeling. I remembered other American friends, teachers, administrators, people engaged in various forms of relief service, missionaries of other church organizations—not many, about a dozen. None of them had any political connections with the U.S. government as far as I knew. They were just faithful servants of God. I fervently hoped that they would be safe. I would avoid at all costs mentioning their names. What an awful business this kidnapping is!

After lunch—another sandwich, this time canned tuna with slices of pickle, and a can of Pepsi-Cola—the two interrogators returned.

"How are you?"

"Okay."

"What do you need? Aspro? Medicine?"

"No, I'm okay. But I think I have an eye infection. Last time, the doctor told me to use Terramycin eye ointment. Can you get some Terramycin eye ointment—a salve? You know, in a tube, for my eyes?"

"Terramycin. We'll see."

"And a Bible—the *Injil.* Holy Book. I need to read the Bible."

"We'll see. Tell us now the names of people you know at the American Embassy."

"I told you, I don't know any. No matter how many times you ask, I don't know people there."

"Well, you think about it and let us know."

They went out and, so far as I could determine, I never heard from them again.

My thoughts returned to the graphic symbols of yesterday: the creative arm of God, the listening ears, the knowing eye, the dove of new life, the support of faith-linked gifts, and the shuttered community of saints. But were there not other images to be discovered?

I looked up at the wall behind me and for the first time noticed three small angular pegs driven into the plaster. Probably pictures had once hung there with familiar faces. What could I imagine there in those three places? Three—a trinity. That's it! Father, creator of heaven and earth, and all there is, my creator who gives me life and reason for being; Son, the full expression of the love of God, come into our human circumstances; Divine Spirit, the very presence of God, "closer than breathing, nearer than hands and feet," now communicating with my spirit. Lord, help me remember and learn the message of those three pegs! Three in one.

My glance moved back to the radiator, and I began noticing its construction. It was divided vertically into sections, but also horizontally, as well as front and back. I began counting the units and they totaled something like 84. A goodly number. Quite a crowd, all gathered together, doing the same thing all at the same time. Just like the saints before God's chorus: singing, dancing, glad as a hallelujah chorus praising the Holy One for his goodness and ultimate triumph over pain, disappointment, and evil.

Against that background of unseen reality I could consider responding to my interrogators more clearly. Apparently they knew little about me, or they would have been more specific in their questions. They asked about medicine, so they must want to keep me alive and in good health. They certainly didn't press hard for information. I'm surprised at their mild approach. I can't tell what may follow, but for the present they seem to be feeling around, trying to learn something. I'll keep a low profile and not volunteer information or get involved with them. But it certainly would be a relief to have something to do.

Another day was about to pass away. How many more would there be in this place?

6

"Ben is sharing in the suffering
of a people who have been subjected
to every kind of violence."

For the first days following Ben's capture I tried to avoid publicity. I had been warned at the American Embassy that I should maintain a low profile. It would be advisable not to go to the news media. I accepted their advice and separated myself from any contact with the press. However, friends soon convinced me that it might help to get Ben's release if I provided information about his identity and his work. Maybe the kidnappers didn't know who he was.

Therefore, I supplied information on Ben to the press so his captors would know something about the person they had taken. I also agreed to an interview with *Life* magazine. The article, entitled "The Last Americans," appeared in early August. It was an account of U.S. citizens who stayed behind in Lebanon after most others had left. The full-page picture of me is startling in the grief, sadness, and pain it captured.

The day Ben was kidnapped I asked a colleague to send a telex to the Program Agency in New York City. This is the structure of the Presbyterian Church (U.S.A.) that is responsible for the church's overseas work. The telex got lost on someone's desk. However, Rev. Frederick R. Wilson, Associate General Director of the Program Agency, received a phone call from Beirut, telling of Ben's capture and expressing the belief that he would soon be released. Fred immediately contacted the State Department on our behalf.

The day after the kidnapping I told Dr. J. Oscar McCloud, the General Director of the Program Agency, that I had been advised by the embassy to keep out of sight. They assumed that church people would only confuse the situation. I suggested that no one publish our recent letters to the United States or make conjectures about Ben. I did not know whether my husband was dead or alive. I hoped he was well and feared that publicity might somehow jeopardize his position. I lived in uncertainty in the midst of a confused situation.

From the first, our Presbyterian church staff in New York and

Atlanta were eager to be of assistance. I was in touch with Fred Wilson by telephone at least once a week. He assured me that the church was ready to stand behind any suggestions I might have as to how they might work on behalf of Ben. Fred remained my contact with the church throughout the long months of waiting. I was pleased to have him as the person through whom to communicate. Ben and I had known Fred and his wife, Betty, from seminary student days and throughout their service in Iran. He shared the perspective of the American missionary living overseas and would understand my desire to stay in Lebanon to stand with the people there in their own days of uncertainty and despair. Fred proved to be a pastor to me and my family, encouraging us, listening to our concerns, and reflecting on the day-to-day struggle to find meaning and clarity in the events in our lives.

Oscar McCloud also kept in touch by phone. He was a helpful strategist, ready to consider every effort for Ben's release. I was to become personally acquainted with Oscar and his wife, Robbie, as the months stretched ahead. Gracious and thoughtful, he took time to find resources, field questions, and make decisions.

On the fifteenth of May, Fred Wilson and other church representatives met in Washington, D.C., with State Department officials and the U.S. Ambassador to Lebanon, Reginald Bartholomew. The ambassador assured them that the U.S. government was doing "everything possible to secure Ben's release."

Within a few days, Oscar McCloud issued a church-wide call to prayer for Ben and the other captives.

> In the hours and days since this event, a growing number of American Presbyterians have entered into the agony of helpless uncertainty which has been the daily experience of millions of persons whom God loves, not only in Lebanon but elsewhere in this violent world. Our pain leads us to issue this call for prayer. We pray:
>
>> for forgiveness for our complicity in the political systems and structures which oppress and dehumanize and drive persons to violent expressions of hostility and rage;
>>
>> for Ben Weir's physical well-being, for sufficient spiritual, mental, and physical resource to endure in the certainty of God's love for him;
>>
>> for Carol Weir and their children: Sue, Christine, Ann, and John;
>>
>> for Ben's captors, that they may be freed of anger and be enabled to act with great wisdom and restraint;
>>
>> for ourselves and all who are concerned that our behavior and speech will be characterized by patience, generosity, and the love which casts out fear.

We thank God:

for the efforts being made to secure Ben's release;

for the courage and steadfastness of the many Presbyterians who voluntarily and faithfully participate in Christ's mission all over the world in situations of risk and personal jeopardy;

for the hope we have in the living Christ from whose love nothing can separate us.

On June 2, just three weeks after Ben's kidnapping, the General Assembly of the Presbyterian Church (U.S.A.) met in Phoenix, Arizona. This group has the task of decision making for our whole church and deliberating church policy. I sent a message to the gathering:

I am thankful for so many prayers. Ben and I wanted to live in such a way that we could become part of the hopes and aspirations of the people among whom we lived. Even now, in some way, Ben is sharing in the suffering of a people who have been subjected to every kind of violence in a violent world.

How something that has been broken, stopped, crushed, and killed can offer itself again is not clear. But it happens. The resurrection is a reality and a symbol of this possibility. I appeal to the Presbyterian Church (U.S.A.) to hear with fresh determination the cries of the people of the third world and to reach out to that world.

Secondly, I appeal to you to turn around from primary concern for local issues to face outward once again to the needs of the world.

Thirdly, I pray that you might develop energetically a clear, coherent sense of direction for the mission of the church in the world.

Following the reading of this statement a resolution was passed by the 690 commissioners to the General Assembly.

The Presbyterian Church (U.S.A.) desires freedom for all those who are captive. However, we make special appeal to those who hold the Reverend Benjamin M. Weir precisely because he is a man who has dedicated his life to the service of God. The man of religion has always been respected by the three monotheistic religions. The release of the Reverend Benjamin Weir will prove to all that this time-honored principle still holds true today as it did in the days of Mohammad.

Sue, John, and Ann went to this meeting. Each spoke to the Assembly about Ben's captivity. Sue described what she thought might be his situation. "He may be blindfolded, he may be bound. He may be in solitary confinement. He may be chained to a bed."

She went on to describe her father as easygoing, friendly, and diplomatic. John noted that Ben and I had stayed in Lebanon to express our hope for peace. Ann spoke of Ben also. How delighted

I was to hear later of their participation. It is no easy task to address a thousand people. Apparently they spoke feelingly, pointing out the need for our country to deal with the underlying political causes of such violent acts as the kidnapping of Americans.

At the time of that General Assembly, there were three bills before Congress that proposed moving our American Embassy in Israel from Tel Aviv to Jerusalem. Our General Assembly had once before opposed this move. The Reagan Administration and the United Nations also opposed this action. Jerusalem was an occupied city and deemed a holy city by not one but three faiths. Relocating the embassy there might be seen as favoring the nation of Israel and the Jewish religion over Islam and Christianity.

Sue, John, and Ann, from their background of many years in the Middle East, were able to join in the discussion of this issue. I was proud of their participation and grateful for their willingness to speak out for their father and for peace in the Middle East.

7

"One more mistake on your part and you're dead."

On the third day of my captivity, I awoke again to the twittering of birds. This time there seemed to be a flock of them, and they continued their conversations for a long time. As I listened, I was again thankful for another night of solid sleep.

On the one hand, the chirping reminded me that I was not completely isolated from the world of nature. Outside these walls were wind and trees and birds, whose singing voices kept me in touch with that reality and took me beyond my closed-in space to remember and worship my Creator and theirs. On the other hand, I recognized my bare existence. Aside from shirt, pants, and socks, I had nothing of my own. I was stripped down to the essentials, completely dependent on God.

At the same time, God was not only the source of meaning but the giver of life itself. Without him I was nothing—a goner. That was true in an immediate sense: each meal was a gift, each day a token of his concern, my health and mental stability a sign of his sustaining care. It was also true in an ultimate sense. If I were to be delivered, it would be because God noticed me and set in motion persons and events outside this room. If I were not delivered, my death or continuing captivity would also be in his hands. In a very existential way I recognized that I belonged to him. I could only try to praise him, as I did now from the heart.

In some ways this was an unnerving thought. It was just God and me without any cushion in between. No distractions. No busyness as an excuse for lack of time. No people to confer with or to act as intermediaries. I was not so sure I could risk exposing myself to God, or that he would find me worth listening to.

Underneath this speculation was a bit of pride that I had made it thus far through life. Now I would have to admit my full and complete dependence on him.

I could also praise him with my body as I exercised. In an un-

Presbyterian fashion I counted "One, two, three, hallelujah; five, six, seven, praise the Lord!" I was glad that my body worked, that I had vigor and spirit. I reveled in the sense of motion even within limits. I was determined to exercise frequently both to break the monotony and to overcome drowsiness. I vowed to spend thirty minutes or more each day working up a sweat in the early summer heat. I didn't want to sleep all day and then remain awake during darkness. In controlling the pattern of my time alone I was retaining my freedom.

I examined myself, partly out of curiosity, partly to be sure I was all right. The soreness of the first day was diminishing and the hurts were mending. Patches of subcutaneous yellow had appeared on my legs; the tight bands of plastic tape had left bruises after all. My neck was still tender, and as yet I lay only on my back to protect my painful chest muscles. But these discomforts were minor. I was glad to have come through the "mummy ride" so well.

I studied my calendar: it was May 10, the birthday of our daughter Sue. Carol and I had been barely nine months in Lebanon when we traveled from our home in the south to the mission hospital in Tripoli, where Sue was delivered in friendly but somewhat rustic surroundings. In contrast to our blond first daughter, Chris, Sue was a brunette like her mother. Now she was thirty: married, working in Santa Barbara, California, fun to be with, warm and affectionate. How I missed her! In my head, I wrote her a letter, telling her exactly how I felt. With tears in my eyes, I sang "Happy Birthday" and saw her, in my mind's eye, blowing out all thirty candles. Even in isolated imprisonment my family was still with me.

I was beginning to find a pattern to the comings and goings of the guard. In the early morning after I was awake I could hear him yawn and hum a tune and then go to the bathroom. He would brush his teeth, clear his throat, and run the water. At first, I thought he must have a heavy cold; it finally dawned on me that he was going through ritual ablution, washing his arms and legs and rinsing out his mouth in preparation for morning prayer. If I listened carefully I could hear a distant Muslim call to prayer: five times between sunrise and the hour after sunset. This seemed to indicate that I was among Shiite Muslims, like the community Carol and I had lived in for five years when we first came to Lebanon. My guard must be very devout.

After he performed the first prayer of the day, I could hear him take his pistol belt from the shelf, check his weapon, and then presumably buckle it around his hips. He would unlock a door, go out, lock it behind him, and tramp down the stairs. After quite a long time he would return, unlock the door, enter and put his parcels down, then lock the door securely. There was obviously no way through that door without a key. Later in the day he went out again for several hours, often not returning until the sunset call to prayer. During these times I could expect not to be interrupted.

When the guard came back, he would bring newspapers with him and would spend long periods reading, for I could hear the rustling of pages and the muffled sound of a radio. Often he would be accompanied by a friend, who would also read the papers and comment occasionally. They would laugh and joke until the evening was gone and then the friend would leave. All this was going on in the room next to mine, but only indistinct sounds came under the door. Once I heard the visitor call the guard "George," which is a common Christian name but hardly one used by Shiites. I guessed it was an assumed name. Another time I heard the guard call his friend "Hasan," a common Shiite name and probably authentic. Otherwise they lived in their world and I in mine, without conversation.

On this day, George came to see me. "You speak Arabic?"

"I know some words," I answered evasively. "I know some words: *marbaha* [hello], *banadura* [tomato], *khubz* [bread], *maiy* [water], *kaneesi* [church], *Injil* [gospel]. But I don't speak Arabic perfectly [that was true]. I need the *Injil.* Can you get me one? I like to read it every day during prayer time." I thought he would understand this kind of need. There was a pause and then he said, "That is not possible. I don't have the *Injil* and I cannot get it." Then he went out. But I was determined to press my request. How much it would help me in my pilgrimage and give me much-needed guidance and assurance!

Later that morning when I was taken on my daily trip to the bathroom, George let me go in alone and stood guard at a crack in the nearly closed door. He said, "Take off your mask when you wash. Put it on when you finish." Even that bit of freedom was good news. I washed my face, neck, and arms with soap and water. The towel next to the basin was filthy, as was the floor. So I once again drank deeply, wiped my hands on my shirt, and adjusted the mask over my eyes.

That same afternoon someone other than George came to see me. He may have been one of the pair that came two days earlier, but he was not Tobacco Breath. Again he took me through a series of questions.

"What your name?"

"Benjamin Weir. I'm a pastor."

"You speak Arabic." Not a question but a statement.

"I know some Arabic words."

"No, you speak Arabic good, very good."

"I don't speak Arabic perfectly."

"Maybe you make mistakes, but you speak Arabic good. You been in Lebanon long time. From 1935."

"No, from 1953." I laughed. They had obviously read newspaper articles about me that mentioned my background in Lebanon.

"That right. We know who you are. Now you speak Arabic. Only Arabic. No more English." With that he proceeded to emphasize his point in Arabic, and from then on I spoke only in Lebanese colloquial Arabic. It made communication much easier for both them and me.

The visitor ventured some comments about my family and activities. He knew about my wife, my children, my role as a pastor, and my teaching at the seminary. He was not acquainted with the Arabic-speaking Protestant Synod, nor did he know the difference between Catholics, Greek Orthodox, and Protestants. But it was clear that he and others of his group respected me on three counts: as a religious leader and man of faith, as a teacher, and as an older person. I found a bit of humor in that last category; I didn't consider myself decrepit and in fact longed to be active.

However, I understood the cultural pattern of showing respect to persons older than the speaker. Though this might merely be polite talk, I would cash in on any benefits accruing to me. As a further sign of respect, he said that I would now be addressed as *ustez* (professor).

He then asked if there was anything I needed. I repeated my requests for the *Injil* and said if he could not find a New Testament in English I could manage with one in Arabic. I explained where the Bible Society's shop was located and said that the cost would be modest. He promised that he would see what could be done about it.

When he asked about medicine, I thought hard. I repeated my need for Terramycin eye ointment and he took note. As a sudden inspiration, I said I also needed Vitamin C; I had noted a deficiency in my diet. He took note of that too. Finally he bid me a courteous goodbye, hoping that I would not be held long. I responded with a fervent *"Inshallah"*—"If God wills," a way of expressing hope.

The tone of the conversation was as important to me as the content. There was an obvious attempt to show respect and even to encourage hope, however vague. Apparently, the visitor wanted to be accommodating, or at least to seem so. He was solicitous of my welfare. That was a good sign.

No longer was I bound by my own constraint of using only English, but I felt considerable reservation. I still knew little about my captors or their purposes. I would be congenial, responsive, and as direct as I could be. But I would not be unduly hopeful about a positive response to my requests. If I didn't expect too much, I would be protected against disappointment. At least I was not being pressured to reveal names of my colleagues, Lebanese or American, and so put them in danger.

As the time I had been held captive increased, so did my discomfort from the heat. I no longer felt the chill of the first afternoon. The sun was warming my room by the time of the noonday call to prayer, and the temperature continued to rise until sundown.

My woolen pants were increasingly uncomfortable, but I had nothing else to put on. My blue jacket with my precious eyeglasses was returned to me on the third day. I folded it and laid it on top of the radiator, out of the way.

I removed my fat key case from my trouser pocket and stashed it away in a jacket pocket, thinking it might be more secure there if someone went through my pants again. If someone took these keys and knew where to try them, they could gain admission to my office and to the seminary buildings. Both seemed unlikely. Fortunately my house keys were on a separate ring in a plastic bag I dropped when abducted. I hoped Carol had gone back and picked it up.

My shirt was beginning to show signs of repeated hand wipings, and my underwear—well, it was not perfumed with roses. Anyhow, I did not show signs of heat rash, and that was important. I carefully spaced drinks from my pint-sized water bottle each day, so that it would last me until refill time the next morning. Fortunately I was given Pepsi and Seven-Up at lunchtime on two successive days, so I saved the cans for collecting urine and emptied them on my daily trips to the bathroom.

On Friday, May 11, my ears told me that a long-winded sermon was being given at the weekly gathering for prayer at the mosque, even though I could not hear the words. The end of the week was approaching. Sunday would be for me a special day of worship. I decided to observe Communion, so when supper came on Saturday I set aside a piece of bread from my sandwich.

On my first Sunday morning in captivity I awoke thinking of a visit Carol and I had made ten months earlier to Pakistan. Once more I could see Christians coming to church, the women in their colorful and graceful native dresses. I thought of a village congregation seated on the floor singing the gospel story enthusiastically in their Panjabi language and clapping to the beat. I imagined teachers, students, doctors, nurses, patients, public health workers, literacy teams, men in construction projects, seminary students and faculty along with missionaries—all awaking and proceeding to places of worship while I was still sleeping. There they gathered at the Lord's table.

My mind moved westward with the sun: Assyrian, Armenian, Persian-speaking Christians in various cities of Iran, and Arabic-speaking Christians in Iraq coming to worship also. I envisioned people of various cultural backgrounds gathering at an ecumenical center in Kuwait. I was part of this far-flung family, the very body of Christ.

I unwrapped my piece of bread and began the Presbyterian order of worship: "We are now about to celebrate the sacrament of the Lord's Supper." For me the "we" had special meaning. The "reading" from 1 Corinthians 11 with its account of the meal with Jesus took me back to apostolic times.

I ate the bread behind closed doors with the fearful disciples and the risen Lord on that first Easter. When it came to sharing the cup I had no visible wine, but that didn't seem to matter. I knew that others were taking the cup for me elsewhere at this universal table.

As others prayed for me, so I prayed for them and their ministry and mission. It was the longest Communion service I have ever attended.

After breakfast I continued to celebrate with Christians I knew in Cyprus, Greece, Italy, Czechoslovakia, Switzerland, Germany, France, Belgium, Holland, Portugal, Spain, and the United Kingdom. I thought of others I knew in various countries of Africa and in Asia and Australia. Then various countries of Central and South America came to mind, and, last, I recalled congregations and faces at Communion in various parts of the United States.

As night came I recalled how Carol and I had listened to hymns on the BBC's "Evensong" every Sunday evening before dropping off to sleep. So I proceeded to have my own quiet evensong. The hymns came tumbling out one after the other.

Some were "great historical hymns of the church" with resounding phraseology, singable tunes, and consistent theology. Others were gospel tunes or children's songs. I even included a few Christmas carols and Easter songs. Each in some way communicated an aspect of Christian life and faith that was meaningful to me.

I was finally able to settle down for the night with a feeling of trust, comfort, and praise, plus the hope that in a tender way I might again share moments with Carol. This last thought brought tears to my eyes.

On about the eighth day, George came into my room, opened the glass French doors and shutters, and went out onto the veranda. I could hear him walk down to the far end of the porch. I had a bright idea: maybe I could get a glimpse of the outside to see where I was. I lifted my blindfold and took a quick peek. Unfortunately, I could not look out the doorway because I was in the corner on the veranda side. A few minutes later George came back, but he did not close the shutters or the French doors. He went out of the room, locking the hallway door after him. Now I could get a better look. I lifted my ski mask: there to my surprise was a reflection from the outside in one of the glass doors. The image was not clear, but I could see trees and mountains in the distance. I was not in Beirut but looking westward across the Bekaa Valley!

I stretched the chain on my left wrist and surveyed as much of the scene as I could. Through the wavy glass I could make out fields, and a line of telephone poles, and mountains in the distance. I was sure I was looking westward across the Bekaa Valley.

I put this bit of information together with all the other little clues. Trucks and vehicles were passing by on a distant highway. The air was dry and not moist as it would be at sea level along the coast. I concluded that I was not far from the main highway that connects the one major city of the Bekaa Valley, Zahle, with the road to Damascus. But that was all.

At least I am not off in some distant, mountainous corner of Lebanon or close to the border of Syria, I thought. Probably they will keep me in Lebanon for the present and not transport me to Syria. Such a conclusion gave me some comfort.

After a short time, George returned and closed the doors and shutters. I was again encased in my bare surroundings. Some days later he came in and opened the outside doors in the same way and went away. Once again I had a chance to take a look. I enjoyed the blue of the sky, the brown of the plowed fields, the green vegetation, and the quick movements of a bird in a nearby evergreen. This rich experience gave me a sense of enjoyment and freedom, as well as a picture to think of during the remainder of the day. It was a gift I greatly appreciated and hoped to have opportunity to repeat. I was also glad to have an idea of where I was being held.

One night I made what could have been a fatal mistake. Evening had come and I consumed my supper sandwich and glass of tea and stretched out to sleep. Believing George had made his last check, I removed my mask as usual and kept it in my hand. Suddenly there were footsteps and a hand on the door.

I grabbed my mask, put the elastic band over my head, and had just pulled it over my eyes when the door opened. George had seen me with the mask and asked gruffly, "What are you doing?" I replied that I was adjusting my mask. He said sternly, "Didn't I tell you to keep it on all the time? Don't ever touch it!" I thought to myself, That's not a very realistic request.

The next day, to my surprise, he brought a present with my luncheon sandwich: a tube of Terramycin eye ointment. I was also given a handful of Kleenex. This was a wonderful surprise. I guessed I had a touch of conjunctivitis, and my eyes were getting a bit blurry from a discharge. It was not surprising with so much dirt and dust on the floor. I began applying the greasy ointment morning and evening.

The following morning I had just applied the ointment and was wiping away the excess when there was a noise at the door. Again George saw my hands on the mask. He came over and thumped the mask on my face. "Didn't I tell you never to touch the mask?"

"I was just wiping my eyes—"

"Never mind. Don't take it off. I'm warning you."

In spite of my caution, he surprised me with his sudden entry again that evening. I had lifted the mask to my forehead in order to blow my nose. I was just wiping my nose and getting the mask in place when he came through the door. Angrily he demanded, "What are you doing, looking at me?"

"No, just wiping my nose."

"Didn't I tell you before always to keep your eyes covered?" he shouted angrily. "Now I'll show you." He went out and closed the door. I could hear him take his pistol belt from the shelf and then handle something metallic that sounded like bullets. Was he loading his pistol?

I knew the kidnappers were worried about the possibility of being identified. For that reason they consistently enforced the blindfold rule. I shouldn't have let myself get caught with the ski mask out of place.

George returned, opened the door, and came storming over to the mattress, where I sat. He put the barrel of his pistol to my temple. The gun was cool and hard against my skin. He said, "I could shoot you." Then he poked the muzzle at the back of my head and said, "I could blow your brains out." Next he poked the barrel under my chin and snarled, "One bullet and you will be dead. I can easily kill you and throw your body into the street. No one will ask about you. Do you understand?"

I replied, "Yes. I understand that you want to kill me."

"You're right. Don't forget it. One more mistake on your part and you're dead. Don't ever lift your blindfold again." With that threat he strode out and closed the door noisily behind him.

I didn't forget. I took him seriously. I was very careful to keep the mask on my head, to listen even more carefully for footfalls, and to be sure the mask covered my eyes before the door was opened. But I could not accept the prospect of continuous darkness. If I were to keep my sanity, I would have to use my eyes, though with great caution. I also decided that he really did not want to kill me, but just scare me. He and the other guards were making sure that they could not be recognized.

From various sounds I heard, I suspected that other prisoners were being held in the same building. When hot tea was poured into glasses, sugar was stirred in, and I could hear a clinking in the next room as the spoon moved from glass to glass. There seemed to be more servings of tea than there were guards, but I could not tell how many more.

Both before I was taken to the bathroom and afterward I could hear other flushings of the toilet and the splash of water in the basin. When food was served I could hear the guard move from room to room, but I was never sure how many rooms he entered. Were the prisoners Lebanese, Americans, or others? Was there any way to communicate with them? Were they in good health or sick and despondent? I had been asked several times if I needed medicine. Would any of them attempt to escape? What demands were made on them or their families? All those questions were unanswerable. But even without knowing these others or seeing them, I could well imagine their fear, stress, anxiety, loneliness, resentment, and helplessness to be like mine. At least I could pray for them, and I did.

I also thought about our captors, of whom I knew very little. Surely they had needs also. What basic area of mutual interest could I find to interact with them? Perhaps I could help them learn English. This would give me an opportunity to know them, as well as a chance to engage in a creative activity. I began to rehearse lessons I had taught to beginners thirty years earlier and to remember some of the hurdles to overcome.

One day my lunchtime sandwiches arrived rolled not in the usual square of wrapping paper used by Lebanese fast-food vendors but in a small piece of Arabic newspaper. Right away I recognized its importance. When I finished eating I folded it carefully and hid it in a pocket of my blue jacket. Later, when the guard went out and locked the door behind him, I took the newspaper fragment and my glasses from the jacket and began to read what amounted to about a quarter of a page. It was old news, but I didn't mind; it was something to read.

One column was part of a speech about current war conditions in the country. Another was an announcement by the Lebanese government's committee on emergency relief, telling when and where the next distribution of supplies would be in West Beirut. There were advertisements and other notices. Columns on the edges were torn so that only part of each line appeared. I tried to guess at the missing words. At least it was something to do, a diversion, a blessing. I could add it to my rosary.

At other meals, the sandwiches had come wrapped in part of a Kleenex. I saved them, along with the white paper wrappers, for cleaning. Beginning with the second day, I asked my guard for a broom to clean the floor. His answer was always a blunt no. The floor had not been cleaned for some time so that rolls of lint had collected in the corners, under the radiator pipes, and around my mattress.

Each day when it was quiet and safe, I would take a wrapper or two and dust the floor as far as I could reach with my unchained arm. This limited sweep was better than just letting the dust accumulate, and it gave me something to do. On the fourth day of captivity the guard also gave me a paper sack in which to deposit garbage and my pile of cleaning papers. In spite of my work, the dirt beyond my reach increased day by day, some of it coming under the door from the hallway. My environment was certainly not hygienic; I could hear the guards outside my door spitting on the floor. But there was nothing I could do about that. I had to learn to entrust that problem to God.

It was ten days since I had been abducted. The mild spring temperatures had turned decidedly hot. Evenings were pleasant but days— and especially the long afternoons, with the sun beating against the shutters—were wearing. My wool trousers were decidedly uncomfortable and my shirt was stained and smelly. I kept asking for pajamas, toothbrush, New Testament, vitamin C, but no response.

For my own amusement, and to create a sense of closeness, I decided I would write a letter a day in my head to each member of my family. I took great care to make each message as personal as possible. I remembered special past events and shared my innermost thoughts, feelings, and reactions to circumstances. I particularly enjoyed detailing what I hoped we could do together when I was free.

What else could I do to amuse myself? I thought of simple games. My blanket had a plaid pattern that could be a playing surface. I tried using bits of dried bread for a game of checkers, but the pattern did not adapt to the requirements of a checkerboard. I tried something simpler: tic-tac-toe. I played against myself until we both knew all possible combinations. Then I tore the cornered top off a pyramidal fruit juice carton, subdivided some drinking straws, and practiced dropping them from a height into the opening. I learned it was much more fun thinking up the games than playing them.

To me the idea of spiritual growth included all these things: games, fantasies, reactions to sounds, images, fears, joys, resentments, scripture, prayer, and worship. Nothing was excluded from the domain of my relationship to the Father. Prayer was becoming for me those times when I sought consciously to live in the presence of God. This meant that I both listened and spoke, as well as waited.

One aspect of growth came to mind because of two seminars I had attended the previous year: learning about myself through the examination of dreams. Carol and I had tried to keep dream journals, but once back in Lebanon I had found little time for it. Now I had that time.

So I began trying to awaken slowly in the morning, in order to be aware of my dreams. It didn't always work, but the more care I gave to it the more I discovered. I found little in the way of exotic or erotic images that would have delighted Freud. Rarely did I remember terrifying nightmares upon waking.

What I did uncover were pleasant party experiences, family celebrations, banquets and buffets with interesting and friendly strangers. I also experienced each of our four children as infants or toddlers: playful, affectionate, cuddly.

On several occasions Carol and I were with students on an outing or a retreat, enjoying their company. At other times she and I were alone sharing experiences and affection. Deprived as I was of human company, the loss was being made up psychologically during sleep. I found I could also enjoy these dreams in my waking hours. This I received as an unexpected gift of God.

There were other surprises, too. One day when the time came for my daily trip to the bathroom, George announced that today I could take a shower but I must be quick. This was tremendous news! There was even a bit of soap in the washbasin. I was delighted at the feel of shower spray on my skin and amazed at the waves of muddy water descending to my feet. I was filthy! The towel provided for drying was the ever-present dirty one. I couldn't touch it. Never mind. I wiped down with my hands, used my shirt to dry as best I could, and dressed quickly.

Back in my room there was a second surprise: a clean pair of loose-fitting cotton pajamas MADE IN CHINA. I could hardly believe my eyes. Once I had put them on, George came in to chain my wrist. I thanked him for the comfortable new clothing. Then I reminded him about the New Testament and the vitamin C. He made no reply, but when he brought a breakfast of bread and olives with a bit of cheese and the usual glass of hot tea, he dropped into my hands a small object.

After he went out I looked, and there in my hand was a small box labeled VITAMIN C. Inside were ten vitamin C tablets manufactured in France. Matters had decidedly changed for the better! But weren't these gifts also a sign that I would be here for some days to come?

Later in the day I had a third surprise. George entered, dropped something on the floor, and said simply, "Keep this next to you." When I lifted the mask I saw a pair of brown plastic slippers. I tried them on; they fit. I took them off and put them neatly next to my mattress on the floor. My spirits lifted; I felt like a kid with a new pair of shoes. Now I could go to the bathroom and back without getting my feet dirty.

That afternoon when the guard took his daily time off, I inspected my vitamin C box. The descriptive paper inside was written in both French and Arabic, so I studied it, trying to identify as many of the French words and phrases as I could decipher. Then I worked with the Arabic, which had a number of words and phrases new to me. At least I was learning something and finding diversion from boredom.

In the box of Terramycin eye ointment I found a similar paper, but this one was written in extremely small print, both English and Arabic. Even so I struggled with it until I heard George insert his key in the outside door and turn the noisy lock. That meant my recreational reading was at an end for the day, but I felt good about my growing library: a piece of newspaper and two drug package inserts. Not much, but far better than nothing.

At sundown before my evening hymn sing I added to my rosary list of blessings three pieces of paper, two slippers, a pair of cotton pajamas made in China, and a shower bath. "If God so clothes the grass of the field which today is alive and tomorrow is thrown into the oven, will he not much more clothe [and provide for] you, O ye of little faith? . . . Do not be anxious about tomorrow, for tomorrow will be anxious for itself." I was trying to learn that lesson in simple ways.

At the end of May a very important change took place. George was replaced by two guards. I really didn't regret the change, even though I had come to know something about George in a very limited fashion. In the early days of his guardship he let slip the fact that he was in love with the study of physics. He had attended the Lebanese University and done so well academically in three years that he was recommended for further preparation in physics after graduation. He had even hoped for a scholarship to study in the United States.

Then, to his disappointment, the Lebanese government ran out of money and the prospect of a scholarship vanished. How he happened to join this armed faction I never knew. However, I guessed that some of his time off may have been devoted to further reading and study. He and I never developed a relationship even bordering on friendship. He showed strong disapproval of what he interpreted as my attempts to lift my mask to see him. Increasingly he was curt, distant, and abrupt. A capacity for violence lay just beneath the surface.

The two new guards were quite different. They joked between

themselves, even engaging in occasional horseplay, listened to the radio by the hour, and were cordial toward me. One of them would occasionally tell me ahead of time what kind of sandwich would be served for lunch and would ask me if I liked the food, even though there was no choice. The other guard said he was interested in learning some English. This suggestion sounded good to me. I proposed we begin that day. When he made no response, I was disappointed.

On the day of the changing of the guards, another man came to see me. He seemed to have some authority. He asked how I was getting along and if I needed anything. I said as far as my health was concerned I was doing well, but that I would like very much to go home. I also told him that I was in need of the *Injil,* the Gospel, in either English or Arabic. I repeated again the location of the Bible Society where he could get a Bible. He was surprised and pleased that I not only could converse in colloquial Arabic but could read classical Arabic. He said that maybe he could find an Arabic New Testament. He said he had looked at one once and might send it along. I welcomed his consideration but did not count on receiving the book.

However, the next day I mentioned my need of the New Testament to the more dominant man of the new pair of guards and made it a point to remind him daily. At first he listened without comment. A few days later he replied, "Well, maybe." A few more days and he mused, "Mmm. Perhaps." A couple of days later he said, "I have a New Testament at home. Be patient and I'll try to get it for you." I was patient, but I also reminded him gently every day. I was beginning to think it was all polite talk and nothing more.

I was now into a daily routine, with the days adding up one after the other. Each morning I would study my calendar carefully and move one space forward in my mind so I would not lose or gain a day. On Fridays, as confirmation, I would hear the mosque prayers and sermon. This confirmed my orientation to time. For me the week began with Sunday, always a special day to anticipate.

As the first days of June passed, I began to realize that there were two different ways to regard the passage of time. One was to regret each day as freedom lost, twenty-four hours of my life span spent without profit. This was true. I did yearn to be active. I also longed to be close to Carol and in touch with my family. However, to concentrate on this kind of regret would only be frustrating and depressing.

Perhaps practical faith and hope and the will to survive required a different point of view. So I chose to add up the days with a sense of achievement, insofar as possible. At day's end I would say to my-self, "Well, you made it through another day, now you must have strength for the next one."

As the light dimmed I would sing to myself, "Now the day is over. Night is drawing nigh. Shadows of the evening steal across the sky." And I would in my heart thank God for providing me with resources and stamina beyond my expectation.

In the morning, I would thank God for another day of living, refreshing sleep, sound body, and expectation of his sustaining pres-ence. After my first exercise period, I would do my Bible "reading," recalling passages that came to memory. I reviewed various psalms and fragments of them. I would choose each day a figure from the Old Testament—Abraham, Isaac, Jacob, Joseph, Gideon, Samuel, Saul—and tell myself his story of faith.

I tried to reconstruct the account of Jesus from his birth to his resurrection from the dead. I detailed the travels of the apostle Paul, adding with mental pictures those places in the story that I had visited. I was astounded at Paul's persistence in the face of obstacles and dangers; I returned again and again to the verse in Romans 8:28, "In everything God works for good with those who love him, who are called according to his purpose." This assurance was the foundation for my grip on sanity and hope.

On the thirty-fifth day of my captivity, in the afternoon, my door opened. I heard the guard come in, walk toward my mattress, then turn and leave. Why? Once the door was locked I lifted my mask to look. I couldn't believe what I saw. There in front of me was a dark blue plastic-covered Arabic New Testament! I was so overcome with emotion that I picked it up in both hands and kissed it.

I opened it and recognized immediately that it was a new transla-tion, the result of seven years of work by a group of scholars and church leaders who included Protestants, Greek Orthodox, and Catholics. My friend Bill Reyburn had coordinated the effort. For the first time, I would have time to read through the entire volume and let it speak to me. I was overwhelmed.

I was also protective. I was afraid that George might return, be displeased, and take it away. So whenever there was a noise in the hallway outside my door I would hide the New Testament and put my glasses away. However, at every daylight opportunity I would read, from early morning to sundown.

Parts of the New Testament letters were rough going because of some new vocabulary. But as I read and reread the pages of scripture for seven months, I found a message on nearly every page. Much of the time paragraphs and whole pages seemed to be written just for me. More than once I felt in company with those first- and second-century Christians who heard the words for the first time. My appreciation deepened for the writers, the compilers, the translators and editors, the scholars and publishers who had made the scriptures available in our day. Above all I experienced the divine Spirit illuminating and communicating the good news.

On the second day of my reading, I was shocked. The book was practically new but as I thumbed through it a slip of paper fell out. I picked it up; it was a scrap torn from a copy book. Several short lines in Arabic were written and then copied a second time. But they were not taken from the New Testament. They read: *Holy war is one of the doors to paradise.* Who had written these words? How had they found their way into this book? What went through the mind of the penman? I could only speculate, but I was sadly aware that the words conveyed a message sharply divergent from the good news.

The Arabic word *jihad* was used in the note to express the concept of "holy war." This definition comes from the use of the word in the Koran. By itself, it simply means "effort," "serious endeavor," or "major undertaking."

In due time I found this Arabic word and its derivatives used several times by Paul in his correspondence. Never did it express a threat or sign of aggression. Rather, it called for "the endeavor of love" or "the serious effort" to communicate and live out the good news. What a contrast! And what a calling!

With the new guards the situation improved further in little ways, but each was an event. One morning at breakfast one of the men asked, "Would you like to drink milk?" When I said yes, he poured a small cupful of warm, sweetened milk into my glass.

It tasted good and was a welcome change. The next day, he gave me another cupful in a large plastic bottle. After he had left I read the label; it was whole milk bottled and sterilized in France. This kind of milk seemed to me fancy and expensive, since most people like ourselves bought the cheaper powdered milk. I said to myself, "These fellows have money to spend, and they are giving attention to my nourishment—as well as to their own."

The bottle itself was also useful as a convenient receptacle for urine. This added gift provided an important source of comfort within the restrictions of my bathroom time.

Once again I was feeling sticky and dirty. Weeks had gone by and I was still wearing the same pajamas. I asked for a shower but was told the water supply was low. Every day I could hear one of the guards go to the roof to check the level in the cistern.

At long last, a month after my first shower, the guard announced when it was time to go to the bathroom, "Today you can have a shower." What a joy! "Take your underwear to put on after you wash your pajamas." What a double joy! So I trotted happily in my slippers and found a large fragrant bar of German bath soap waiting for me.

To my surprise, the shower water was warm and I proceeded to scrub down with vigor. Then with equal zest I used the soap to wash my pajamas until the water turned brown. I washed my clothing a second time. After a determined rinsing and wringing of pants and jacket, I was finished. At last I was clean. I was also surprised to find myself tired from stooping over the bathtub. Yet, it was good exercise and I felt alive.

As I had been instructed before entering the bathroom, I put on my mask and knocked on the door to signal that I was finished.

The guard said, *"Na'aaman"* ("Good health from a good bath").

I replied with appreciation, *"Yin'aam 'aleyk"* ("Good health to you too").

He asked, "How long do you suppose you were in the bathroom?"

"Maybe twenty or thirty minutes," I guessed.

"Over one hour," was the reply.

I was surprised but glad I had been allowed to enjoy that simple pleasure. I was also pleased that he had not been pushy like George. A few days later a further unexpected boon was the presentation of a toothbrush.

I was beginning to feel a bit friendly toward my guards and decided to follow up my earlier suggestion. So I said to them in turn, "Would you like to study English with me?" I was thinking of myself and my need for activity as much as of them.

The more retiring one, whom I supposed was also the younger, said, "I haven't much schooling and I don't know that I can do it."

I answered encouragingly, "Never mind. You don't have to read. I'll teach you by talking." However, I could tell that he lacked courage and incentive. This realization made me feel sad that he was passing up an opportunity for a helpful educational experience.

The dominant guard responded positively to my offer. "I began studying English in secondary school, but I've forgotten a lot. I'll bring a book and you can teach me."

I was a bit crestfallen, because I wanted to begin with oral pronunciation. I had no choice but to make the best of the opportunity. A few days later he brought his book for me to see. It was *English for Beginners.* Knowing I must teach blindfolded, I memorized the first and second lessons and thought up pronunciation drills. Two days later we went through it together.

Then there was a space of a few days, and a renewed beginning. Then another space and a third feeble attempt. After more delays and excuses for not continuing, I realized that he was not a very motivated or serious student, but it did bring us together in a marginal way.

Much of my life had been fueled and revitalized by the opportunity to reach out to others. Part of the torment of my captivity was that being a prisoner I could not serve someone else or interact with another person. Yet I had prayer. This was becoming more and more a concrete way to serve with those far away.

8

"They may be small, but they make a lot of noise!"

When the American ambassador, Reginald Bartholomew, returned to Lebanon, I easily obtained an appointment. I was picked up at the seminary in a bulletproof car. The driver and escort were kind and sympathetic. We drove down to the British Embassy building, where our embassy was now housed. Several tanks lined the road, manned by marines and bristling with weapons. The car stopped and was examined (both in the trunk and underneath) to make sure it was not equipped with explosives. We continued on through a maze of tank traps, or "dragon's teeth." It would be difficult for a car bomb to get through *these* defenses!

I felt strange and uneasy in this car. Here were the streets of Beirut where my family and I had walked freely and safely, day or night. What had brought American citizens to this low point? When we first arrived in Lebanon, there was dissatisfaction with American foreign policy, true, but there seemed to be little resentment toward individual Americans. Even now the fundamentalist extremists insisted that they did not dislike Americans, they only felt that the U.S. government was working against Islam, particularly in its support of Israel. But anti-American feelings had grown steadily through the years until Americans were now barricading themselves behind concrete barriers and hiding in their homes and institutions.

The short drive brought me to the embassy. I was ushered through tight security, up back hallways, and into the presence of Ambassador Bartholomew. He was gracious and repeated how concerned the government was about Ben and the other hostages. He assured me that they would do the utmost for Ben's release and asked what organization Ben was working with. "The Presbyterian Church," I replied. There was no response. I thought he might not know anything about our church, so I added, "It is a small denomination."

"A small denomination?"

"Yes, compared with the United Methodist Church or the Southern Baptist Church."

"Well, they may be small, but they make a lot of noise!"

We laughed together. I took his comment as a compliment and was pleased that our church had the reputation of having the courage and the integrity to speak out on issues of importance to us.

I left the embassy deeply depressed. There appeared to be no new developments. Ambassador Bartholomew had assured me, however, that a special envoy was on his way to Lebanon who would conduct a complete investigation. I could only hope that this promise would bring results.

My family decided that I should not be alone in Beirut over the summer. Our youngest daughter, Ann, had accepted a position to teach elementary students at the Schutz American School in Alexandria, Egypt. On her way to her post she could meet our oldest daughter, Christine, and come with her to visit me in Beirut. Chris, working in Saudi Arabia, would take some vacation time and meet Ann in Athens.

The Beirut airport was closed because of fighting nearby, making a direct flight to Lebanon impossible. Instead, Christine and Ann could fly to Cyprus and board a boat for an overnight trip to the eastern Beirut port of Jounieh. Our church people on the eastern side would meet the boat and drive them to the Green Line, the artificial boundary dividing Christian-controlled East Beirut from Muslim West Beirut. From the other side of the Green Line, they could get a Muslim taxi driver to take them to our apartment. I prayed that God would protect them on this uncertain journey.

How delighted I was to see them as they stood at the bottom of the stairs waiting for me to unlock the gate! I couldn't control my tears. After forty-five days alone, it was wonderful to hug members of my family and feel their presence.

Chris had visited us from Saudi Arabia at Easter time, just a month before Ben's capture. She had previously spent two years at the American University Hospital in Beirut, teaching in the nursing school. She had also worked in the emergency room during the desperate days of the Israeli invasion in 1982. Her contacts in Lebanon and her fluency in Arabic would be very helpful.

Ann, our bright and creative youngest, always offered sensible comments, emotional support, and perceptive, thoughtful suggestions. Ann was setting off on the new adventure of her first teaching job.

My morale zoomed to new heights immediately upon their arrival.

I gave a prayer of thanks for their safe arrival. We were now a team, facing the challenge before us.

Both girls had grown up in the neighborhood of our apartment and had walked to and from school and work alone. All these years, we had not been afraid to be out in the street at night. Things were different now. Something menacing had been added to our beloved Beirut. Neither of the girls felt comfortable on the streets of their youth. In fact, very few foreigners now lived in this vital crossroad city of the Middle East.

The sense of a quiet, stable, cosmopolitan city was gone. Many of our friends had left for safer parts of the country or had returned to their native lands. Other people simply took over their vacant apartments. All around us, apartments were now occupied by these newcomers. Some people were in genuine need of housing. Many just came and demanded the more comfortable apartments of others, requesting huge sums of money before they would leave. It is amazing how compelling such an appeal is from someone who has several companions carrying submachine guns.

However, I was convinced that we women would not be kidnapped. After all, I was with Ben when he was forced into the car. They could have taken me at the same time, but they didn't.

I felt safe in the apartment now that I had the companionship and wisdom of my daughters. It had been very hard for me until they came. During the frequent shellings, I would hide in a stairway area we used as a shelter.

Our apartment had a veranda off the front of the building. It overlooked a lovely garden, maintained by the people in the first-floor apartment. Their own house and business office had been destroyed when a mosque next to their home was demolished in the bombing.

This garden plot was special for us. Understandably, keeping a real garden was not a top priority in these troubled times. Yet it still had some large old pine trees which shaded the apartment on hot summer days. Our veranda offered a sheltered place to sit. We often had our meals there, catching the evening breeze off the sea. In fact, a tiny porthole-sized section of the Mediterranean was visible. How I loved this veranda! The girls and I spent most of our time together there.

In the evenings when there was no electricity, we placed a Butagaz lamp on the table and the girls and I played Scrabble and other board games while the sounds of war rumbled in the distance. We plotted and planned. Whom should we see? Where should we go? We sifted through ideas, information, scenarios, and schemes. We went over and over this perplexing problem of Ben's captivity.

We attended worship regularly during the summer, both Arabic and English-language services. In spite of the frequent shelling, we found that the bombardment of our area occurred mostly in the afternoons, allowing us a relatively safe morning to get to church near our apartment.

Church services were difficult times. Tears were always just below the surface. The first Sunday after Ann arrived was particularly difficult. When the prayer was offered for Ben, she was so overcome with emotion that she had to leave the service until she could regain control.

What caused such emotional outpouring by the three of us? Was it a reminder of Ben's absence from worship, since this act of faith always took the highest priority with him? Perhaps it was the genuine love and concern for him expressed by the community. Although we found worship a tender time, these ties with the community of faith were essential. We needed to worship God with all our faith questions in the midst of a community that confirmed God's faithfulness and presence at all times.

In July, the husband of an acquaintance I had met in California when we were home on leave six months earlier phoned and asked if he could visit us. Of course! Christine was at home, and she and I eagerly awaited the arrival of this tall, handsome young Muslim. He had been visiting his family in Baalbek. We were delighted to hear that his wife had asked him to help in Ben's release.

He said that through a friend who had contact with the group who held Ben he had learned that they were very determined. The captors were Lebanese Shiites influenced by the revolution in Iran. They would free Ben only upon the release of the seventeen prisoners held in Kuwait or by direct word of the Ayatollah Khomeini. We were elated to hear that this young man was willing to go to Saudi Arabia or Kuwait to intercede for us, but he needed the cooperation of our government to facilitate visas and travel plans. Would we go to our government to get their cooperation?

Here was a concrete offer of help from someone who could try to negotiate Ben's release. However, I had to tell him that we didn't have much influence with our administration. He said that the group would not like this news; they were hoping we could make contact with our government. Fortunately, we did have an appointment with Ambassador Bartholomew that day, so we asked the visitor to meet us later, after he concluded his Beirut errands.

At the embassy, we relayed the whole story. Would our government cooperate with this young man? Ambassador Bartholomew said he couldn't make a decision without consulting Washington, but he did not give us much hope that our government would agree. Sure enough, word came back to us that Washington was using "quiet diplomacy" of its own. They did not want to get involved in anyone else's effort.

We returned to our apartment and sadly relayed the government's negative response to our new Muslim friend. He said that he would still see what he could do for us and suggested that Christine go to Baalbek. She was excited by this idea. She was convinced that if she could tell the captors how much Ben understood the despair and pain of the Shiite community, they would release him. Her Arabic was the most fluent among us. Should she go?

The road to Baalbek was unsafe. There had been several kidnappings, casualties, and murders. Should we take a chance? I vetoed the idea. At least, we should not do it yet. We would consider the matter and keep in touch.

In the meantime, I visited the Lebanese Education Minister at his office. Any word about Ben? He told me he had good news. Ben was alive and well. The case was being considered at the highest level in government. He advised me to call back in one week. I waited that week, hoping against hope. Then I called. He was sorry, he said. The problem had become internationalized. If I needed any help locally, he would be glad to be of assistance.

As I searched my mind for an influential person who might help us I thought of the Rev. Jesse Jackson. He had been successful in winning the release of Airman Robert Goodman from Syria early in 1984. During Jackson's campaign for the Democratic presidential nomination, his foreign policy statements showed concern for people of the third world. I felt that he was appreciated for his perspective by many in Lebanon and the Middle East.

I wrote to the Rev. Jesse Jackson at his Rainbow Coalition headquarters and asked for his assistance in obtaining Ben's release. Susan and John had been in touch with Rev. Jackson's office in Chicago, but they had not talked with anyone in authority. But Jesse Jackson was in the midst of his campaign for the Democratic party's nomination as candidate for President of the United States. Our concern would have to wait.

9

"Oh, God, I don't want to die.
I want to live. I want to be free,
to be useful!"

June dragged on, hot and boring. Most of the day I would sit without my pajama top to lessen the effect of the heat. Occasionally a guard would open the glass door and the outside shutters. This would allow a slight breeze, especially in the late afternoon, to creep under the locked door and even to rattle it a bit. I welcomed any diversion.

The hot weather made me thirsty. Having been told the very first day that the tap water was safe for drinking, I would cup my hands and swallow as much water as possible on my daily trips to the bathroom. The guards noticed this, since tea was their normal beverage, and asked why I drank so much water. When I told them how thirsty I was in the small hot room, they brought me a 1½-liter plastic bottle of cool drinking water, saying I could have more when I wanted it.

This was very good news. It indicated both human and divine care. In the imagery of the Twenty-third Psalm, I was like a thirsty sheep at noonday being led to "still waters." I was also discovering a new appreciation for the concrete, specific, common items of life: pajamas, drinking water, slippers, bread.

One especially hot noon, the guard came into my room and found it stifling. Of his own accord, he opened the inside glass door, leaving the outside shutters closed. That permitted a delicious breeze to circulate through the crack under the locked door to the inner hallway. However, it also brought another surprise. Once the guard was out of the room, I lifted my blindfold and noticed that there was a reflection on the glass of the open panel of the French door.

I wondered if I could see myself and if I could risk a look before the guard returned. I stretched my chain and moved to the foot of my mattress. The glass was wavy so that the image of my face was indistinct, but still I could see myself for the first time. What a change! I had begun to grow a full gray beard, the first in my life. And my hair was beginning to hang shaggy over my ears. What would Carol say? To my surprise the beard was not an even color but patchy, between gray and white. The truth came home: It was great to be alive, but I was no longer as young as I once was. Maybe the leader's respect for my age was encouraged by what he saw.

That afternoon I heard the sounds of other men coming into the building. They were greeted and there was talking, so apparently they were other guards. After quite a while my door was unlocked and someone came in.

The person entering my room came near me and asked how I was. Then he gave me pen and paper and told me I was to write down a message he would dictate. Following his orders, I took my glasses out of my jacket pocket and turned my back. My ski mask was taken off, and I put on my glasses.

He began, "To his Eminence, the Prince of Kuwait," and proceeded word by word and phrase by phrase. I thought to myself, Why am I writing to the ruler of Kuwait? This text is going to sound cockeyed, translated a phrase at a time rather than as a whole.

The dictated message complimented the ruler, saying that since he was motivated by humanitarian concerns, he would surely accept my plea for the release of the seventeen men held in prison in Kuwait. The note asked for his mercy; I was being held because of these men. Whatever happened to them would happen to me. I would only be freed if these prisoners were freed. I was instructed to state that when these seventeen men were released, I would be released from my "hellish" conditions.

Here for the first time was the reason for my kidnapping. I had suspected that it was related to other political factors, but what were they? Now it was clear that I was being held as a hostage to assure the safety and release of the seventeen Shiite extremists in Kuwait.

I remembered reading about the bombings of the French and American embassies in Kuwait some months earlier. My daughter Chris had written us at the time from Saudi Arabia, telling of the anxiety that this event created there, but I had not paid much attention to the arrest and trial of these radicals. Now I suddenly found myself directly related to them and their destiny. These were "the political reasons" mentioned by my captors in May.

I was appalled by the news. I began to sweat. How could I ever be delivered from this dilemma? I could not imagine that the Prince of Kuwait would be swayed by my plea. American influence would be key to any change in Kuwait. Would our government make any adjustments in its confused Middle East policy now?

My thoughts were further frustrated because I did not expect the release of these men, if they were indeed bombers. In addition, I knew the Reagan Administration had taken a "no negotiations" posture with respect to all hostage situations.

As I turned the full implications of captivity over and over in my mind, I could see only a continuing impasse, at best, with this situation dragging on for months or years; at worst, I could imagine the captors losing patience or becoming infuriated at the lack of response and deciding to execute me. In their eyes, I was a pawn on a chessboard, without significant value. "Oh, God, I don't want to die. I want to live. I want to be free, to be useful!"

When the brief letter to the Prince of Kuwait was completed to the satisfaction of my mentor, he said to my surprise, "Now you are going to read it." He blindfolded me again, unlocked my chain, led me into an adjoining room, and told me what to do. My blindfold was removed. I was placed in front of a masked man holding a video camera and given a newspaper to hold in front of me, with the text of the letter on the back. When he snapped his fingers, I began reading; when I finished, I closed my eyes. I was told to do it again. Then someone replaced my blindfold and I was led back to my room.

Later I could hear low voices and then someone reading in the adjacent room. I assumed that other hostages were making appeals on the same videotape. It all seemed so contrived. I could not imagine a positive response from video-recorded messages.

Once I had said my piece into the camera I was led out blindfolded, but not back to the same room. We walked down a short hallway, through a creaking door, and into a different room. Once the door was closed I found myself seated on a rolled-up mattress.

As I lifted my headgear and looked around, I found scratched on the wall above the radiator a crude calendar with rough additions of dates and a clear total of "111 days!" I was shocked by the realization that the previous occupant had been confined here nearly one third of a year.

To one side was a rather elaborate outline of an Eastern Catholic cross, expressing faith and hope. I accepted that message with gratitude and prayed that whoever put it there would be sustained, wherever he or she was now. I wondered how long I would be kept in this new place. It was stifling hot and made me wish for a drink of water and the relative comfort of my familiar room. After some hours, I was led back to my usual surroundings.

As the days went by, and I tried to decide how many other captives, if any, were being held in the same apartment building, I realized that I was occasionally hearing a woman's voice. When George was relieved of his duty and the two new guards replaced him, I learned something more. I could hear them occasionally, in the evening, talking with a person in one of the back rooms of the apartment building. On one or two occasions, I could hear them laughing and joking. I could hear a voice answering them. I was sure that it was the voice of a woman.

A few days later one of the guards said, "Tell me about the principles of psychology." I said to him, "Psychology is a vast study. It has many different aspects. I cannot tell you about the whole field in a few minutes."

I asked him why he wanted to know about psychology. He said, "There is a woman here who is in low spirits. She does not have much inner sense of stability. She misses her two children. I want to know what to do to cheer her up." I suggested that he might just try to listen to her to determine what her real needs were. He could then encourage her in this way. After he left, I could hear her vomiting in apparent distress. So I began praying for her, hoping that she might be released and be able to return to her family.

Only a few days later, I was suddenly removed from my rather large room and returned to the much smaller back room where the sun beat directly against the shutters. There was mud caked to the floor. Furthermore, the chain that bound me to the radiator was much shorter and it was attached to my right wrist, giving me much less freedom of my more useful hand. But at the same time, I was aware that the woman had been moved from her back room into my front room where she would be closer to the guard and there would be more of a sense of activity. How ironic! I had prayed for her relief and this meant giving up my room so that she would have a more pleasant place. I thought to myself wryly that God really does take me at my best intentions.

It turned out that I was actually delighted to be moved on this particular day. The guards had brought some recorded tapes which they were playing. The tapes were very long chants which went on for an hour or more. They were repetitive chants done in a singsong, and although I couldn't hear them clearly enough to understand the words, they were loud enough to be very irritating. After hours of this sound, I tried to plug my ears, but found it hard to get relief. I began to feel that this endless sound was too much. "How much longer can I take this?" At this point, the chanting stopped and they moved me to the back room. That was a decided relief for which I was grateful. As I reflected on this, I realized that in this strange answer to prayer God really seemed to know what was best for both the woman and myself. It also enforced my belief that God has a sense of humor.

When I was moved into the smaller back room, the guard said to me, "There is one rule you must observe. You are not allowed to stand or move off your mattress to the side of the room." On the far side were French doors closed by a shutter that I was not allowed to open. But as the day went by, I decided to take the risk.

That night, when I thought the guard would be asleep, I got up carefully and stretched my chain to its maximum length. With my left hand I opened first the inside panel of the French door and then the outside shutter. I could see stars overhead and, off in the distance, the dim lights of a town. Nearby were some buildings of the village. I had been mistaken in assuming that I was near the city of Zahle. In fact, I was a considerable distance from there, much farther north in the Bekaa Valley.

To see the out-of-doors was indeed a treat. Carefully, I closed the outside shutter and the French door and lay down. I cherished the memory of what I had just seen and my curiosity was aroused. I also realized that I could indeed open the shutter and get a view. I decided that I would do this again in spite of the danger. The next night and several successive nights I repeated this same operation. I was rewarded with visions of the starry sky and once of the silver moon.

After a time, I realized that I could probably look out very early before the guards were up. The next morning I was awake before the first call to prayer. I could make out the outlines of the distant hills and mountains etched on the horizon by the rising sun. This meant that I was on the eastern side of the valley, right up against the foothills of the Anti-Lebanon Mountains. I closed the shutter and the French door.

I lay down and waited. I could hear the guards getting up and preparing for morning prayers. Later, when I assumed that they had gone back to sleep, I opened the door and shutter once again.

The sun was touching the tops of the distant mountains. The world was coming to life in a pink haze. On a nearby slope, someone had planted a fig orchard. I looked down over the rooftops to see green poplar trees pointing skyward from a depression I took to be a small valley. Farther to my right I could see green fields and, still farther in the distance, the Lebanon range, which was beginning now to receive the morning glow. I was grateful for this reminder of the beauty in the world outside.

That picture enchanted me. I would rise each morning and look out my window, repeating to myself the words of the psalmist: "I will lift up my eyes unto the hills."

One morning I was looking out my window when I heard sounds outside my door. It was a guard looking into the room next door. As quietly and quickly as I could, I closed the outside shutter and nearly closed the inside French door. I sat down on my mattress, but there was no denying that I had been looking out my window. A new guard had come on duty and was checking out the hostages. He asked me angrily why I had been at the window. I told him that I was curious about what was outside. He was irate and scolded me harshly, but he did not strike me. He went away, but after a while he returned with another guard. They both said that I had put my life in jeopardy. I knew they meant it. To my surprise, the whole day passed without any reference to the incident. However, at midmorning of the next day, a new guard came and spoke to me. He scolded and condemned me, telling me never to let it happen again.

In the middle of the following day, I heard a guard come into my room, approach my bed, and say nothing. I was curious about what this meant. I wondered if his approach might be related in some way to the previous incident. Without warning he raised his arm and brought it down on me, but with no force, in a symbolic kind of beating. He repeated the gesture several times; then he stopped.

I said to him, "Why did you do that?"

"You know why," he replied, and went out of my room. That was the last I heard of the incident. I was lucky to get off so easily.

There were other reasons why the guards were sensitive about my looking out the window. There was more to see than the beauty of nature: a machine gun emplacement a short distance away. Occasionally there was the chatter of a machine gun nearby during the day. I realized that the noises came from this gun emplacement. Also on the top of a nearby hill I could see pointing skyward the long barrel of antiaircraft artillery. When reconnaissance planes, which I assumed to be Israeli, would pass overhead, I could hear the *chug-chug* of antiaircraft guns from the surrounding hills. The nearby gun was one of these weapons. This meant I was being kept in an area where organized forces of Iranian revolutionaries were located. It did not become clear to me what the relationship between my Lebanese Muslim captors and the Iranian revolutionary forces was. Even so, I was sure that my Lebanese captors could only keep hostages in that area with the knowledge and permission of the Iranians.

One of my concerns was the obvious possibility that a major conflict might develop in the area where I was being held. I could imagine bombing by Israeli planes of our building and that I would have no escape because of being chained in my room. I also realized there could also be a violent attack by those Lebanese who opposed the Iranian revolutionaries and it might engulf my building. There was no way in which I could deal with these dark scenarios. I could only entrust myself to God to see me through whatever might take place. Time and again I had to surrender my anxieties to the Almighty. God would know best.

Ten days after preparing the letter to Kuwait, the same man came to me—at least I supposed him to be the same one. He said that there had been no response to the first recorded message. He sounded frustrated. "What state in the U.S.A. do you come from?" I told him California. He asked me who was my "parliamentary representative" from that state. I was not able to name him. I hadn't voted there for a long time. He couldn't believe that I didn't know my representative.

Then he wanted to know who in the American government would pay attention and champion my case. I could not think of anyone. He was getting impatient. He urged me to give this matter serious attention, for my life depended on it. This threat was not very reassuring, to say the least. Finally I said, "I don't know anyone of influence in the government or in politics, but I'm sure that the Presbyterian Church leaders will make a determined intervention on my behalf in Washington."

"All right," he said, "then write a letter to them. I'll tell you what to say and you put it into English." Once again I turned my back to him, took my glasses from the pocket of my jacket, and put them on after my headgear was removed. I was handed a notebook and ballpoint pen and prepared a letter similar to the earlier one, but I addressed it this time to the Rev. William Thompson, Stated Clerk of the Presbyterian Church (U.S.A.), and Dr. J. Oscar McCloud, General Director of the Program Agency.

Again I held a newspaper and read my letter in front of a masked cameraman. I could only hope that the message would get through. At least it would tell Carol and my family, and those friends who knew I was kidnapped, that I was indeed alive. Certainly my beard and long hair would be a change for them! But I had little hope that they could do anything effective toward my release.

10

*"He is alive.
You must be very happy."*

In July someone from the embassy telephoned and asked us to come down to the ambassador's office. "We have something to show you." What could it be? We went, of course, all three of us.

Ambassador Bartholomew and Dianne Dillard accompanied us to a room containing a videotape machine and showed us a tape that had been made of Ben. There he was, pale and tired, with a shaggy beard and long hair! He was holding a newspaper dated July 5, 1984.

He read a statement that said he was being held in exchange for seventeen prisoners imprisoned in Kuwait. The tape was addressed to the head of the Program Agency, Oscar McCloud, and William Thompson, whom Ben thought was still the Stated Clerk, the two people who might have authority to act in the name of our church. The statement urged them to press the American government for the release of the seventeen prisoners because Ben's life was in danger unless these men held in Kuwait were released.

Apparently Ben had made some mistake the first time he read the statement. He was asked to repeat it. This time when he finished the statement he quickly shut his eyes. I thought to myself, they must be keeping him blindfolded; the light is hurting his eyes! But he did have his glasses; I was glad for that. As he read the statement a second time, there was a catch in his voice, a hint of deep emotion. He must realize how difficult it would be to meet the conditions for his release, I thought.

"Well, he is alive. You must be very happy." The embassy people expected us to be pleased with the tape, but I was depressed. Ben looked so constrained and weary.

Ambassador Bartholomew said that their people had studied the tape. Ben did not appear to have been tortured. I was grateful for that, but I was immediately concerned about the demands. Was the State Department in touch directly with the Kuwaitis, actively seeking Ben's release? I was assured that our government was involved in "quiet diplomacy" and advised to tell no one about the tape, especially not the media. "Your husband is in danger, and any publicity might cost him his life. If you say something, he might be killed."

They offered to show us the tape again, so we watched it another time. During one of the rewinding procedures, the operator went a little too far, and we saw someone else holding a newspaper! Quickly the tape was moved to our segment. So, there were others. Were they with Ben? Were they held in the same building? Could these people include William Buckley and Jeremy Levin? I had never met them, but I knew they had been kidnapped too.

The girls and I also noticed that Ben's wedding ring, simple symbol of our love and commitment, was missing.

Where had the tape come from? How did the State Department get it? Ambassador Bartholomew refused to say. We had been shown the tape only for verification, to learn if it was really Ben.

I wanted Sue and John in California to see the tape too, and Sue made this request of the State Department. Couldn't a copy be sent to California for them to see it there?

No, for security reasons Sue and John would have to travel to Washington, D.C. Our government was not going to let any copies of the tape out of its hands.

When Sue and John viewed the tape in Washington, they too were surprised by Ben's appearance. He looked okay to them, and it was obviously Ben, but he had never had a beard before, and his long hair was strange. They noticed that when he read the part that said he would be killed if the demands were not met, he stumbled.

Sue and John found themselves with a few extra hours before flying back to California. Knowing that I had previously written to the Rev. Jesse Jackson for his help in obtaining Ben's release, they decided to visit his Washington headquarters. They arrived as the staff was dismantling the office. Rev. Jackson had withdrawn from the race for his party's presidential nomination.

In the midst of this hectic activity, one of the staff, Jack O'Dell, sat down with John and Sue and listened to their story. He was genuinely interested. Susan and John were delighted by this warm welcome. At last they had been able to reach someone with authority. (Apparently my earlier request for help had not arrived at the Washington office.) Jack O'Dell said they would be glad to do whatever they could to assist in the release of the kidnapped men. John and Sue returned to California feeling that at last they were beginning to make some progress. In our weekly telephone call Susan suggested that I make a formal request for the Rev. Jesse Jackson's official participation in the hostage issue.

I wanted the church officials to see the tape also. The State Department refused. I insisted. The tape was addressed to them, after all. Why was the State Department being so difficult? Finally it was agreed that the Associate Director, Fred Wilson, could see the tape. James Andrews, the new Stated Clerk, was denied the right to see it.

Chris, Ann, and I decided to go to Damascus to make a personal appeal to President Hafez al-Assad of Syria. Perhaps he could exert some influence over those holding Ben and the others. We knew that Muslim fundamentalists were permitted to enter the Bekaa Valley through Syria, that the Iranian Revolutionary Guard functioned in and around Baalbek, and that Syrian troops were stationed in eastern Lebanon. Perhaps President Assad would help us.

The Beirut airport was now open—a good sign. It was agreed that we should fly to Cyprus to meet Fred Wilson and confer with him there. From Cyprus we would fly to Damascus. Chris and Ann had Syrian visas already, and my Lebanese Identity Card would allow me to buy a Syrian visa at the airport.

The trip to Damascus represented a new approach for us in seeking Ben's release. A Lebanese professor at the seminary helped me prepare a letter to President Assad. I was told by Syrian friends that he was especially willing to hear pleas brought to him by women in need. I decided not to work through our embassy or go with officials from our church. We would make the visit as a family in trouble seeking the release of our husband and father.

This journey to petition the help of others also marked our unspoken conclusion that we would no longer depend on the "quiet diplomacy" of the U.S. government. While we continued to work with government officials during the months ahead, there was a constant awareness on our part that they could not or would not come through for us at key points of practical and emotional need. Perhaps this is the mark of governments everywhere.

The Damascus road was my first real step into the world of political lobbying. Assertiveness would become my strength and sole weapon in the battle I was to fight. It is significant that my family and my church were my support on this maiden journey into the world of politics.

We had an easy trip from Beirut to Cyprus. The beauty of this island was stunning after our many months in ravaged Beirut. We took a cab to our beachfront hotel and had a lovely swim in the sea. Excited and pleased to meet Fred, we were filled with expectation and hope. We did some catching up at dinner, but I kept looking over my shoulder the whole time. Was anybody overhearing our conversation? Were we being observed?

The next day we headed for Syria. Ann could only stay three days in Damascus because according to our plans she was to report back to Fred in Cyprus. Chris was to leave Syria and return directly to Saudi Arabia because her vacation leave was almost spent and she could spare only a few more days.

We expected to be on our own and had planned to stay at a Syrian Catholic monastery. But we walked off the plane to be met by U.S. Embassy staff, who helped us through the airport customs without delay. Well, we had intended to avoid the embassy but there was no way we could do that now.

We took a taxi to the monastery and found the accommodations inexpensive, adequate, and friendly. We could actually get hot meals! My room, with TV and a fan, became our meeting place.

We telephoned the U.S. Embassy for an appointment with the ambassador. Then we followed through on a couple of church contacts we had been given in Beirut, but no leads developed.

The next day we were graciously received at the embassy. Ambassador Rheu knew of Ben's plight from a previous telex I had sent him. I had been directed to him by friends for any assistance I might need. However, he was leaving the next day for the United States and a different assignment. He wished us well and introduced us to an assistant, the Deputy Chief of Mission, April Glaspie, a very gracious person. She said she would try to obtain an appointment for us with the Syrian Foreign Minister. We had tried unsuccessfully on our own to get the appointments we wanted, so we were glad to accept her help.

Since the phone at the monastery was not working, Chris, Ann, and I spent the next day making telephone calls from the Sheraton Hotel, where we had lunch. Progress was slow, but we were able to reach some friends who might help us. We had visited Damascus many times as a family during our years in Lebanon. Standing on the edge of the desert with the Barada River running through it, the city has always impressed me as an oasis—a bustling city surrounded by beautiful but bare hills.

On this visit we saw pictures of the president, Hafez al-Assad, all over the city. The Samiramis Hotel where we had stayed during previous visits was now a headquarters of some sort for Iranians in Syria. When I stepped into the hotel to ask for directions, I noticed that the lobby and halls were filled with pictures of the Ayatollah Ruhollah Khomeini. We also noted busloads of women in Iranian-style dress in the city. These were new features in Damascus. What exactly was the relationship between Syria and Iran?

On Sunday we were to meet the Greek Orthodox Patriarch in Damascus. We arrived just after the worship service and were ushered into his office. He greeted us warmly, gave us coffee, and told us how sorry he was about Ben's abduction. He reminded us that the United States was most difficult in its relationship with Syria. How well we knew! He promised to get in touch with President Assad on our behalf and asked us to return for his answer later that day.

I felt this man was personally concerned. He knew Ben and seemed genuinely to wish for his early release. The three of us were so happy after this meeting! We made our way down the street called "Straight" and thought of the passage in the Book of Acts about the apostle Paul. Maybe we were about to see a new light in our journey of darkness.

But when we returned that evening, the Patriarch met us on the stairs in front of his office. He told us he had made the contact and would do his best for us, but there was a vagueness about his response. The edge of possibility he had shared earlier was now gone. We didn't seem to be getting anywhere after all. We thanked him for his effort and left. Ann was to return to Cyprus the next day to report to Fred. Chris needed to go back to her job in Saudi Arabia.

No appointment with President Assad was yet forthcoming. I decided to stay on in Damascus and continue my efforts. The girls left together on Monday. That same day I received word that I could meet with Foreign Minister Farouk al-Shirra on Wednesday.

Before seeing the Syrian Foreign Minister, I was graciously received by the Deputy Foreign Minister, Miss Kanafani. We talked together at some length. She reiterated that Syria could not accept the agreement recently forged between Lebanese President Amin Gemayal's government and Israel—an agreement, as we both knew, that had been encouraged by the United States.

At the time of Lebanon's independence in 1946, Lebanon had agreed to make no foreign alliances without the approval of Syria. Any such alliance between Lebanon and another government could put a foreign nation at Syria's border. I understood the Syrian perspective, but the long discussion was wearying, and I was anxious to meet the Foreign Minister. However, after an hour of talk we found to our surprise that we had mutual friends, and both of us enjoyed swapping news about them.

Miss Kanafani accompanied me to the meeting with the Foreign Minister, who spoke excellent English. He assured me that his country did not know who had Ben or where he was being kept. He told me they were greatly concerned about Americans being held. He assured me that Syria was willing to help in any way, but he reminded me that his government was not able to control all actions in his own country—let alone in Lebanon. There had in fact been an unsuccessful assassination attempt on the life of the Syrian vice-president shortly before my visit to Damascus.

When I asked if I could see President Assad, the Foreign Minister said he was not sure it would be possible. I had the feeling I would never make it to the President's office, so I gave the Minister the letter I had written, and he promised to deliver it. I had gotten as far as I could.

I made my way out of the building, walked directly to the U.S. Embassy nearby, told them I had decided to leave Damascus, and accepted their help with plane reservations. Arrangements for the short flight to Cyprus were quickly made.

The next morning I got up before daylight and hailed a cab in the darkness of early morning. (The cab driver said I spoke Arabic like a Russian and seemed surprised that I was an American.) In the airport lounge I was greeted by an official-looking young man who glanced at my passport and then offered me a seat out of the early morning sun near his desk. We chatted for a while in Arabic. His English was not very good. He shot all kinds of questions at me. "Where are your children?" "What do they do?" "Where was I going?" They sounded innocent enough, but a little out of place.

When I left my chair to go toward the plane, the same young man went with me. He wanted to take me through security and introduce me to the stewardess. This was a little more attention than I was used to receiving. I thanked him but declined and said I would stay with the other passengers in the waiting room. When I boarded the plane, there stood the same young man again. I asked him laughingly what he was doing there. He said that he had arranged a good seat for me and was checking to see that I was properly cared for. It appeared that the Syrian security police wanted to see me safely out of the country.

In Cyprus, I reported to Ann and Fred, who had decided to stay to hear about my visit with the Foreign Minister. We needed to talk face-to-face. Fred thought his telephone was tapped, and I suspected that my Beirut phone was also being monitored. I reported my impressions of the visit. I told them I felt that the Foreign Minister was sincere, and perhaps we could count on Syria's help.

Fred headed for New York, and Ann and I spent another day swimming in the beautiful water of the Cyprus coast before heading back to Beirut. Ann would have to leave for Alexandria shortly. How grateful I was for her companionship! Our intimacy and sharing as two adults would come to mean a great deal to me in the days ahead.

11

"Why doesn't your government do something?
You are a forgotten man."

August proved to be very hot. Toward the end of the month to my surprise a book appeared in addition to the Arabic New Testament —a well-worn student copy of *Romeo and Juliet.* Although the cover was badly torn, the inside pages of the text were clear and had good notes. The introduction by a professor of literature in England was still intact and gave a good background to the play. As I read through the volume, once, twice, and a third time, I came to see Shakespeare's classic drama as the interaction between two families caught in the throes of civil conflict. This spoke to me of the tragedies of the Lebanese civil war, which had been going on for a decade. I saw Shakespeare's two young people in love both as victims and as signposts of a solution to this conflict, and I prayed with new fervor for the resolution of Lebanon's agonizing troubles.

In the course of the following weeks several other books appeared. Although some were hardly worth reading, I was grateful for those that provided food for thought. George Orwell's *Animal Farm* was charming as a description of the way in which a revolution eventually becomes oppressive. For the first time I read Albert Camus's *The Plague* and found in it a most thought-provoking question about how to deal with human suffering. It spoke not only to my own situation but also to the suffering the Lebanese people were passing through at such great cost. Through the significance of being present with people in their fearful and ambiguous and agonizing hours of suffering, I was reminded that God suffers with us during these extreme circumstances.

There was also a paperback propaganda piece from China entitled *On the Long March with Chairman Mao.* Although the little book was written to glorify the Chinese leader, it portrayed not only the great suffering but also the solid determination of Chinese revolutionaries to create a new society. In the midst of it all there was the human will to survive the long march, the terrible winters, sickness, and displacement. The stalwart determination of so large a number of the Chinese people gave me courage to be persistent.

There were many times when I was frustrated by the behavior of the guards. During the hot days of May and June I was often very thirsty and without adequate water. When I asked a guard for water he would say, "All right," but it was always an hour or more before he brought it.

Usually I had enough to eat, although mealtimes were very irregular. Sometimes food would be delayed as much as two or three hours. I remember one whole day without anything to eat. At other times, a meal, especially an evening supper, would be skipped without explanation. These were frustrating times for me, not because I was hungry but because meals were a very important part of the rhythm of the day. I was frustrated not only by missed meals but because explanations were either flimsy or nonexistent. On one occasion a guard apparently forgot to buy bread for the day. In a Lebanese family this is a serious matter, because bread is the main part of the diet. However, the guard tried to hide his failure by saying he wanted me to appreciate the fact that poor people did not have enough to eat. And it was true that the food I was receiving, both in quality and quantity, was better than many poor Lebanese Shiite families have. I had no reason to complain.

More frustrating was the way in which the guards aroused my expectations of freedom. Almost from the beginning they would say, "Don't be anxious. You will soon be free." I soon came to realize that they did not know; this was just polite talk. At other times someone would say, "You are stuck here. Nobody cares about you. Maybe you will be here one year, five years, or ten years. Who can say?" And on one occasion a guard said to me, "Why doesn't your government do something? You are a forgotten man. No one asks about you. No one cares about you. Your government has nothing to say."

"I know that I am not politically significant," I told him. "Perhaps my government is not asking about me. But I know my church. I am sure there are people in the Presbyterian Church who are working actively on my behalf. Perhaps you do not read of their efforts or statements in the newspapers, but I am sure they are genuinely concerned—and concerned not only about me but about all people in Lebanon who are suffering."

One of the most frustrating experiences came after I was moved into the back room, where there was no light after nightfall. In the larger front room I had been able to see by some light that filtered in from next door, where the guards gathered. However, in the rear room, when food was brought to me after dark it was hard to see it.

One evening the guard brought me a dish filled to the brim with noodle soup. I said to him, "Can you give me a candle so that I can see to eat this?" "No," he replied, "there is no candle." And he went out. I tried to hold the bowl near my mattress and then raise it to my mouth. However, in the dark I could not determine when the bowl was level, and I succeeded in spilling a good deal of it. What a mess! A few nights later I was given a spoon in order to manage these situations better.

One of the guards gave the impression that he wanted to be friendly. However, his behavior proved very erratic. Frequently he would come into the room, saying with exaggerated friendliness in a high-pitched voice, "How are you? Are you happy? Do you want to go home? Maybe you will be here a hundred years!" His interest seemed superficial, and I was irritated by this nonsensical behavior, but there was nothing I could do about it.

12

"Pray, yes,
but we must be active also!"

The days seemed to drag by. The Rev. Habib Badre, Professor of Church History at the seminary, had suggested that I visit his uncle, Dr. Charles Malik. This veteran politician had represented Lebanon at the founding of the United Nations. He had also held political office in Lebanon and had been a professor at the university. He was a good friend and a seasoned diplomat.

One Sunday, I went to see Dr. Malik, driving across the Green Line to the east side of the city. I was always uneasy crossing this imaginary line. I could vividly remember the time when I was driving with two women from the East Side, where we had attended church, to the West Side, where we lived. As we went along, I noticed that there were no other vehicles. Something was wrong. Suddenly a jeep came speeding up, cut in front of my car, and pulled off the road. The jeep was filled with young men. They looked at us, but they didn't move. I was extremely nervous. I didn't say anything to my passengers; I just kept on driving for another quarter of a mile to the other side. Then I breathed a sigh of relief. I learned later from friends that the crossing point had been closed by sniper fire just ten minutes after we passed through.

This Sunday, all seemed clear and calm as we drove up the hilly area outside of Beirut proper.

Habib Badre and his wife were there to greet me. Many other people came and went from that house, seeking advice and help for the multitude of problems facing the Lebanese community.

Dr. Malik and his wife talked with me. We were served coffee. Dr. Malik knew Ben well and expressed his concern. "You or your church officials must go to your government," he said. "Get an appointment with Secretary of State George Shultz. Don't take no for an answer."

I phoned Fred Wilson and relayed the message. He agreed to put a request for such an appointment in motion. The reply came back from the State Department: "No appointment." *I continue to hope that you can see Shultz,* I wrote back. *I was advised not to accept a negative answer.* Fred tried again and met with the same rejection. Even the Moderator of the Presbyterian Church, Harriet Nelson, was unable to get an appointment with our Secretary of State.

Fred Wilson and the Stated Clerk, James Andrews, finally did get to see Richard W. Murphy, Assistant Secretary for Near Eastern and South Asian Affairs. "We don't know who has Mr. Weir or where he is," the Assistant Secretary told them. He added that the demands being made were not simply a life for a life, and therefore any negotiations would be tough. Fred came away from that meeting very discouraged. It seemed that the hostages were not anywhere near the top of Mr. Murphy's priority list.

By the end of August I was finding this long wait increasingly difficult. How does one pray? The routine phrases, the smooth clichés, the glib requests do not serve. How do I pray for Ben? I agonized as I tried to visualize his situation. How do I pray for the captors? They were acting out of desperation and perceived injustices. I no longer even knew what to pray for myself.

I treasured the verses in Romans which say, "The Spirit helps us in our weakness; for we do not know how to pray as we ought, but the Spirit himself intercedes for us with sighs too deep for words. . . . God works [or cooperates] for good with those who love God." Isn't it amazing? It sounds as if the initiative is with us, and as we step out and act for good, the Spirit of God will make those efforts productive. To friends who said, "All we can do is pray," I replied, "Pray, yes, but we must be active also!" I wanted every effort made for Ben and the other hostages.

That summer I got over the sense that I had to make myself holy and presentable to God in order to pray. Rather, I presented myself to God as I was, completely dependent, uncertain, weak, full of doubts and fear; hope against hope, faith in search of faith. When I found it hard to hold on to God, God held on to me.

13

"Wishing you a Merry Christmas."

One of my guards was replaced by a younger man. He was very gentle and often asked if there was anything I wanted. Each time he took me to the bathroom and brought me back to be chained in my room once more, he would say as he attached the padlock, "I regret that I have to do this. You remind me of my father, and I want you to know that I respect you. I hope that before long you will be able to go home."

My response was always, "I know that you have instructions and that you are not free to do what you want. I understand."

Sometimes one of the men would be curious about me and my attitude and would ask what I was thinking. "If you were released and had the opportunity someday to recognize me, what would you do? Would you try to capture me?"

I would reply, "No, I don't want to turn you in. Rather, I want you to know that I forgive you and that I hope you will find a more profitable and self-fulfilling line of work. My faith teaches me to forgive."

There was a variety of attitudes among the guards. One would be belligerent but later try to make up for it. The one who was mocking and silly didn't seem to know how to relate to me at all. Two or three of the younger men were sympathetic and tried to show it, extending little kindnesses or encouraging me by saying, "You will be going home soon."

This remark was no help because I believed they did not know and were only trying to cheer me up. Officially, the more responsible guards distinguished between me as a person they respected, in contrast to the actions and policies of my government, which they regarded as oppressive and hurtful.

I often wished I could meet these men under different circumstances of freedom and openness. Then I could get to know them as they were in a normal situation. However, the truth was that I was a captive and they were the captors. Our relationship inevitably was mostly distant and untrusting. This posed a dilemma: how to try to understand them, love them, and pray for their welfare.

I had to learn that God knows their inmost hearts as he knows mine. He wants to be merciful to us all. We are all human beings, wanting to live lives of peace and joy. I believed then, as I pray now, that in spite of the ambiguity of our relationship, God wishes fulfillment for their lives. How he will lead them into peace and self-fulfillment I don't know, but I continue to pray that their lives may be filled with his blessing.

On October 4, 1984, I celebrated Christine's birthday. Ten days later I celebrated John's. It hurt not being able to express my love for them directly.

To make a birthday cake for Chris, I took a little cheese carton and poked holes in it. I rolled pieces of foil from the cheese into small candlelike shapes.

I sang "Happy Birthday" several times during the day; I thought about her and wept; I made prayer wishes for her and felt the emptiness and the deprivation of my life. Ten days later I made a cake for John. These imaginary moments with my family stimulated my will to survive. A month earlier I had hoped to be with Carol for our thirty-fifth wedding anniversary. Now I inwardly promised myself, "I will come through this and be with them to celebrate their future birthdays!"

Six months had gone by. One evening after dark, when the weather was turning cool, I heard several men come into the apartment. They talked together and then began moving around, scraping furniture on the tile floor, going in and out. I wondered what all the activity meant. After a long time, a guard came into my room and told me that I would be moved.

"To another room?" I asked.

"No," he said, "to another place."

I wondered where it would be and what it would be like. I worried about leaving these familiar surroundings. I would be leaving "home," with my symbols of hope. Would I have new guards? Would there be less freedom in the new setting?

The guard returned with a plastic bag and told me to gather together my few belongings: jacket and trousers, reading glasses, Arabic New Testament, cup and spoon, bottle of water, and plastic container for urine. As I waited, I heard someone being led out of the room next to mine. Just as I had suspected, there was a fellow hostage nearby! A long period of silence followed. Had they forgotten about me, or was something ominous about to happen?

After two hours or so, a guard came and told me to stand up. He unlocked the chain from my wrist and removed it. He warned me sternly to be quiet "as a mouse": no coughing, no talking, no noise at all.

Then he led me out of the room, down a stairway, and up into a vehicle, which seemed to be a small enclosed truck. At least, this time I was not carried out like a sack of potatoes. He put a blanket over my head and told me to sit. I felt that I was on a cold, hard metal floor.

I moved a little to adjust my position and immediately felt the tap of his pistol on my head. "Sh-sh-sh." Then I heard him step down from the vehicle onto crunchy gravel. All was quiet, deathly quiet. Had something gone wrong? Perhaps I was not being moved to a new house, after all, but being taken out for execution in some lonely place. I could not shake the fear of immediate danger. Had there been some political development that called for punishment of the hostages? Was I to become an example of the captors' seriousness?

It was hard to concentrate. *Lord, give me faith now to trust you. I am yours and in your hands. Whether in life or death, help me to know I belong to you.* I repeated the Twenty-third Psalm: "The LORD is my shepherd. . . ." I was physically on edge, frightened, heart pounding, feeling the chill of the night air. Yet the promise of God was also an immediate encouragement.

After an interminable time, I heard more steps on the gravel and another person climbed into the truck and sat near me. Then a third person joined me. A guard got in next to us. A driver climbed into the front seat, closed a creaking door, and started the motor.

We were off, rumbling down the road, picking up speed, turning corners, bouncing over the bumps but finally coming to a stop. We had traveled about fifteen minutes. One of the hostages was taken out first, then myself. The third hostage was taken out after me. A guard grasped my arm and took me along a short walk, then up some stairs. We entered a building and then a room.

I was led through two doorways and told to sit on a mattress where I could feel a blanket. The voice insisted I be quiet. I would sleep here.

Relieved that this was simply a move to another location, I stretched out with a sense of thanksgiving. Before I could go to sleep, the guard returned with a chain and padlock. I asked to go to the bathroom, but he said, "No. Not until morning." He bound together my two ankles, ran the chain to my wrists, bound them with the same chain, and locked the chain in place. Then he told me to sleep. Such an order was hard to follow. It was impossible to stretch to my full length. I finally managed to lie on my side and dropped off.

In the early morning all was quiet, but I could hear birds beginning to twitter outside. I was in a bare room, perhaps 9 by 12 feet. Papers covered the window. I managed to crawl to my knees, lift a corner of the paper, and peek out. There were trees next to the window, but I could see a few two- and three-story buildings nearby. I was probably one floor above the ground, but could see no way to escape.

I wanted to relieve myself but decided to wait until a guard came. I was getting increasingly uncomfortable. I was also angry at the long delay. At one point I thought that I heard momentary footsteps outside the door and called softly, *"Ya muallim"* ("Oh, teacher," a common phrase to attract attention). There was no response. I was getting a bit desperate. I clapped my two plastic sandals together repeatedly, but got no answer. Finally, I decided I could last no longer and did not want to run the risk of getting my clothes wet.

I managed to crawl on my knees to one corner of the room. After guessing which direction the floor sloped, I urinated in the corner. To my surprise, the stream trickled toward the door and even underneath it. The guard won't like this, I thought, but I can't do anything else. At least, I'm more comfortable now. I crawled back to my mattress, relaxed, and dozed off.

Later I awoke, sat up, and had just finished my morning prayer and meditation when the guard unlocked the door. He was angry and asked what happened. I told him. He tried to belittle me, saying that I was like a child and should know better. I replied simply, "I waited as long as I could. I'm sorry about the mess." I was prepared for a tongue-lashing or beating, but he let it pass and later told one of the other guards to clean the floor.

That night three of the guards came into the room. One asked how I liked being *"makbougsh"*: that is, hog-tied. I replied that it was not comfortable, but I had been able to manage. He said, "We'll fix you up." Then they proceeded with a lot of energy, joking, and loud talking to drag in a long chain which finally they were able to fix to the eye of a reinforcing rod that was poking out of the ceiling at the top of the light cord.

Once the chain was securely padlocked to the eye, it was passed around my two feet and padlocked in place. They had me stand and stretch the chain until it bit tightly into my ankles, making sure I could not reach the window. Then I was left alone once more. At least I could now stand to my full height, use my arms and hands, and exercise more freely. This was my new home.

By late October the hot weather had turned to cold days and nights. The guard had given me an extra blanket which I doubled to keep warm at night. I felt very cold.

As the early days of November approached I hoped the presidential campaign in the United States might work on my behalf. Soon after November 4, a guard said to me, "It does not seem likely that you are going to be released soon. There has been an unfavorable turn of events. You can expect to be here another month." This news was disappointing, but I told myself it might well be more than a month before I saw any positive development.

By mid-November, the weather had turned decidedly cold. To keep warm, I exercised almost every hour. I put on everything I had, including my woolen pants and jacket, over my pajamas. Then a storm came, with thunder, lightning, and hail, and later I could tell that snow was falling outside. The next day when I went to the bathroom I peeked out the corner of the tiny window to see a heavy layer of snow on the ground outside and on the distant hills.

The bathroom itself was a very tiny room with no washbowl, only a cold-water spigot near the floor. When I washed my hands, the water was icy. The toilet was the simplest fixture, a porcelain bowl set in the tile of the floor connected to a pipe that went down to the ground. It was difficult to keep my spoon, plate, and cup clean when I washed them, but I managed.

The primary difficulty was to stay warm. At night I did my best to roll up in my three doubled blankets and drop off to sleep for an hour or two before being awakened by the cold. I would exercise to get warm and then roll up once more and go back to sleep.

In the morning I would hold my New Testament in one hand and read as long as I could. Then I would shift it to the other hand while I warmed the first hand under the blankets. I gauged the temperature by how much fog my breath made in the cold air. I wondered how much colder the winter would become at this elevation of about 3,000 feet.

In early December, to my great surprise and delight, a guard came with new underwear, a pair of fleecy pajamas, and a fleecy jogging suit. In addition there were also a pair of woolen gloves and a pair of warm socks. I was allowed to take an improvised bath, the first good wash-down in a month.

Once I had the new layers of clothing on I found the temperature much more agreeable. In my room there was a hole at the top of the wall that penetrated to the outside. It was intended for a stovepipe, but of course there was no stove. I kept asking one guard and then another please to plug up the hole so the cold air would not come in. For many days, the guards said that it was not possible to close this hole because I needed the air for ventilation. However, one sympathetic captor finally got a big wad of paper and plugged it up for me. This helped to keep the room a bit warmer.

As Christmas approached, I realized that the day would have no special significance for my Muslim guards. However, during the Advent season, I sang very quietly to myself as many Christmas carols as I could. The more I attempted to recall, the more I could remember. I greeted the morning of December 25 with my own quiet Christmas caroling, thinking it the only way I had to celebrate. I recalled past Christmases with my family and longed to be with them on this day of days.

Around noon I heard someone coming so I pulled my ski mask over my eyes, as usual. To my surprise, two sets of footsteps came into my room. One guard moved to one side of me near the wall. Then they both moved behind me. "Face the wall," one of them said. I did so. "Now take your blindfold off." I was very reluctant to do this; I knew the peril of accidentally seeing them. "Never mind. Go ahead and take your blindfold off!"

Very carefully I raised the mask and looked. There in front of me was a large bakery platter with a chocolate-covered Yuletide log cake! Such a Christmas confection is traditional in parts of Europe, and the custom has become common among Christians in Lebanon. However, I was surprised that the Muslim guards had purchased such a cake. The guards said to me, "Isn't that nice?" I told them, "It is amazing!" Then in Arabic a captor said, "Merry Christmas!" He ordered me to put my blindfold back on and took the cake from my room.

After some time the two guards returned. Each put a plate into my hands. When they left I found one plate held a very generous portion of the cake, more than I could eat at one time. The other plate had bananas and very good tangerines.

Shortly after that another man came, who spoke with authority in good English, and who I believed that I had not met previously. He began by wishing me a Merry Christmas. He told me that he and the others did not wish me harm. He hoped that I might be able to join my family by Christmas next year.

"Do you mean that it might be a whole year before I can be with them?" I asked.

"I hope that it will be sooner, but certainly by next year."

I did not find this answer very reassuring. He went on to say that he had brought me some Christmas presents. He put them into my hands, saying, "One small container is a bottle of cologne." Another was a ballpoint pen and a piece of paper. I would be allowed to write a letter to my family. I could send greetings and personal comments but nothing about my circumstances or activities. (This Christmas Day note never reached Carol.)

He told me that I was being held for purely political reasons and that my captors had nothing against me personally. He explained at length their opposition to the U.S. support of Israel. He expressed extreme anger at the destruction caused by Israeli forces during their invasion in 1982, an action that brought death to thousands of Lebanese people and displacement to hundreds of thousands more, especially to the Shiite population of south Lebanon.

Then, with great feeling, he said that he and his fellow Muslims did not want to be regarded as less honorable and less worthy of respect than Christians in Lebanon. I told him that I had many Muslim friends and that I never thought of them with less than great respect. I also explained that for years I was aware of the harm that U.S. policy in the Middle East had caused to many people. I had repeatedly spoken out for change in that policy and was disappointed when no significant change came.

He continued his emotional speech about Muslims being considered second-class citizens in the West. He wanted me to know that a decided change in attitude was necessary. Finally he wished me a Merry Christmas and put an envelope in my hand. After he had gone out I opened it and found a Christmas card picturing Mary, Joseph, and the baby in the manger, with the words *Wishing you a Merry Christmas.*

I was touched by the fact that my captors were trying to make amends for keeping me confined over what they knew was an important Christian holiday, although it was not the kind of celebration I would have chosen. Along with this sensitivity several of the guards mentioned that they too, as Muslims, knew the Koranic story of the birth of Jesus and respected him as a prophet. I was left with two contradictory sets of feelings. I felt they were unjust and misdirected, and I resented that they were holding me as a hostage. At the same time, I recognized that they were trying to show a spirit of sympathy and humanity.

Some days later, in the morning, there was a scraping sound as a guard dragged a metal object into the room. Then he struck a match and I could smell the odor of bottled gas. It was a portable heater! He said he would leave the heater a little while to warm up the air; after perhaps thirty minutes he came and took it away. For that short time it made the room warmer and I was able to take off my gloves. I appreciated this, even though the room was cold for the rest of the day. On a few successive days, the heater was brought into the room again for brief periods. Finally one of the guards said that the bottled gas was too expensive and there would be no more heat. At least there was a hot glass of tea at breakfast in midmorning, and in the early afternoon stew or soup was often served.

At the end of December, I was awakened one night from a deep sleep. The guard said I was to be moved to a new location. After a blindfolded ride in a small car, I was taken out and led inside, upstairs, and into a room. The building was warm compared to where I had been. The guard told me to sit down on a mattress. He then chained my left wrist to a radiator.

After he left, I lifted my blindfold to find that an electric light was burning. I was now in a place very much like the one I had first occupied. I concluded that I was in the same building but in a different room. This situation was much better than my most recent living conditions. The radiator was warm! There was light, and a guard immediately provided a bottle of water and a container for urine. I felt very good about my surroundings and went off to sleep quickly.

14

"You are a religious person. Pray."

In early September, unable to get any information about Ben, I explored the possibility of writing to him. Surely, if Ben was alive, there must be some way to reach him by letter. I had reported Ben's kidnapping to the International Red Cross in Lebanon. They were not able to help me, although they had been given the role of maintaining contact between Lebanese who were kidnapped and their families. "We haven't seen any Americans," they said. "If we did, we would report immediately to the American Embassy."

"Take my husband's name," I insisted. "Maybe you will find out something about him."

"Sorry," they said. "We can't help you."

I tried the Red Cross again, this time through Geneva. I sent a letter for Ben there, asking that they try to get it to him. In the meantime, I tried again through local church contacts to see if a letter might be sent to him, with no success.

I was forced to rethink our strategy. Were we really doing the best thing by being quiet about the whole situation? I discussed the problem with Fred Wilson, and he wrote to Jim Andrews.

> *Carol is thoroughly persuaded that the time has come for greater visibility to be given to Ben's plight. Immediately after her husband's seizure she asked that we all keep a low profile, and we have done so. Now she has become convinced, after months of silence have had their chance, that there is nothing to lose, and perhaps something to gain, by more public awareness.*

As a result, a message was sent to all Presbyterian pastors in the middle of September. "The time has come to call the attention of your own representatives in Washington to Ben's plight. Let no obstacle stand in the way of his release. We also urge you to call upon your people to pray for our forgiveness for our complicity in the political and economic systems and structures which oppress and dehumanize and drive persons to violent expressions of hostility and rage."

Many people were already praying for us. We encouraged others to pray for Ben, the other hostages, and the captors. The presence of others through prayer continued to be a vital part of my strength.

I kept in contact with the embassy staff. Their headquarters had been moved to a new site near our apartment in West Beirut, and for matters of security an annex of the embassy had been established in East Beirut. It was thought that Christian-controlled East Beirut provided greater security than West Beirut, where the bombing of the embassy had taken place and where the kidnappings had transpired.

On September 20 an explosion occurred at the East Beirut annex. Fourteen people were killed and many more were injured. This terrible event made action on behalf of the kidnapped men even more difficult.

Peggy Thomas (the Rev. Margaret Orr Thomas), a staff member of the Program Agency in New York, had lived with her family in Iran for a number of years. She is a bright, active, dedicated person, with the ability to provide a global perspective in discussion, and is a persuasive advocate for all peoples of the third world. Peggy now became involved in helping us. In 1979, at the time of the revolution in Iran, three British missionaries had been kidnapped. Peggy reminded us that it was Terry Waite, a special envoy for the Archbishop of Canterbury, the Right Reverend Robert Runcie, who had successfully negotiated the release of these missionaries. On September 20 I received a note from Fred Wilson.

> *At the suggestion of Peggy Thomas through the introduction of Bob Lodwick, who knows him from World Council of Churches contacts, I talked with Terry Waite on the phone for a most encouraging few moments. He told me that this was the kind of situation they could and would be involved in. He wanted a face-to-face conversation. Bob will provide that by going to London next Monday.*

Bob Lodwick, a staff person living in Geneva, served as liaison between the U.S. church and Presbyterian churches in Europe and the Middle East.

Fred had already sent background material to Terry. Bob flew to London for the briefing. Terry Waite was interested in working with us but totally absorbed by contacts with the Libyan government over

British citizens being held in that country. We would have to be patient.

At the end of September the seminary sponsored a seminar on the island of Cyprus for students before the start of the fall semester, and I offered to be part of the leadership. Hearing of this possibility, the Program Agency staff arranged for our son, John, to visit me there. I was delighted. Because of the kidnapping of American men in Beirut, I had steadfastly refused to allow John to come to Lebanon. But I could meet him safely in Cyprus and have the benefit of his company and aid.

Arriving in Larnaca, I was met by John, who had just flown in from the United States. His luggage was lost, but he was in good spirits and expected his bag to arrive the next day. We traveled to the retreat center; how peaceful it seemed after my weeks in Lebanon! I reported on my activities; John filled me in on efforts made by the family and the church in the United States.

At the end of the conference came a delightful surprise: the Program Agency suggested John and I might spend a few days in Egypt. We could visit Ann and see how she was settling into her new job. I had a feeling my staff friends in New York hoped to keep me out of troubled Beirut as long as possible. Of course, I welcomed the suggestion, and we left for Egypt.

"Welcome, welcome," were Ann's words as we hugged each other. Smiling, bright, and lively as always, she ushered John and me to our rooms. Her own room, just down the hall, was simply furnished. However, she had a few of her personal treasures with her, and I gave her a piece of lace from the beautiful handwork of Cyprus for her coffee table.

This was Ann's first year of teaching, and she was only at the beginning of the school year. Yet I could tell that Ann was confident in her role as teacher. She loved the children and struggled with the poor language skills of the students, several of whom had arrived in her fourth-grade classroom with almost no knowledge of English. Her classroom was full of evidence that she and the students were embarked on many creative and challenging projects. She proudly showed us some of the poetry they had written.

John left after two days to return to California. He had already missed some of the classes he was taking, so he needed to hurry back. I had one more precious day with Ann before heading back to Lebanon and the fall semester at the seminary.

During our last hours together we dreamed about Christmas. Surely Ben would be released by then. We would celebrate Christmas in Egypt, at Luxor or Cairo. Chris could join us from Saudi

Arabia. John, Sue, and her husband, John Nelson, could come from California, and with Ben we would have a celebration to remember.

I returned to Beirut from Cyprus to begin final preparations for the fall semester at the seminary. Continuing my efforts on Ben's behalf, I went to see Ghassan Seblani, a high-ranking official of Amal, the largest Shiite militia. I was a bit nervous. What kind of reception would I receive? Two women met me at the door. They offered coffee and chatted with me until Mr. Seblani appeared. He also talked very pleasantly with me and made me feel at home. He told me that he and his men had tried hard to gain the release of Jeremy Levin but had been unsuccessful. He said that money had been paid to some of his men for Jeremy's release. When he heard about this, he had demanded that the money be returned.

He did not seem to know anything in particular about Ben, but he did say that the three hostages at that time, William Buckley, Jeremy Levin, and Ben, were being held in order to have America negotiate an Israeli withdrawal from the south of Lebanon.

Islamic Jihad had claimed responsibility for the abduction. I understood it was a small group, loosely organized for specific tasks and part of the larger party, Hezbollah (Party of God). The captors were Lebanese but had strong ties to Iran. In any case, Mr. Seblani said the Americans were moved from place to place, sometimes held in the Bekaa Valley and sometimes moved to West Beirut. In fact, he said, William Buckley had been brought to West Beirut some four months ago to be released to Amal, but the kidnappers had refused to hand him over at the last minute.

Could Amal help get Ben released? He would make no promises but he insisted that Amal was not kidnapping Americans. They were against the idea. I wrote Peggy Thomas that, according to Amal, the State Department was not making any overtures to get the Americans released. If Amal was to assist in the release, they wanted some gesture from the State Department.

On October 15, our church appealed to those who were holding Ben and the others. "Examine the long public record of the Presbyterian Church in providing consistent support for efforts directed to Palestinian determination in their homeland and a peaceful Lebanon; examine the purposes and quality of service to the different communities of Lebanon rendered by Benjamin Weir since 1953; examine the effects of these months of captivity on this sixty-year-old man of God, and release him to his family and his friends in Lebanon and around the world."

I had been advised by a staff member of the Middle East Council of Churches office on Cyprus to get in touch with the Druze community in Lebanon. Walid Jumblatt was the Druze leader and head of the Progressive Socialist Party. I had met him before through mutual friends. Now a relative of that staff person on Cyprus drove me to Walid Jumblatt's headquarters in Beirut. There were sandbags and armed guards everywhere, but after identifying ourselves, we had easy access to Mr. Jumblatt's office. He was not there, so I met the second-in-command.

I told my story. Every time I did this I was brought close to tears. It was difficult to present the facts and plead for Ben's life. Mr. Jumblatt's representative said that the Druze were in no way responsible for the kidnapping; it was Hezbollah, the "Party of God," who held the Americans. He seemed sympathetic. Could he be of help? I knew that the area where we lived in West Beirut was under the control of the Druze. He might be able to find out more information about Ben.

The Presbyterian Church continued to explore new avenues for us. We needed the help of the international community. The Reformed Church of France was contacted to ask President Mitterand to raise the issue of the hostages with President Assad of Syria. How I wished the President of the United States would take a personal interest in our case!

On October 26–30, Fred Wilson made a trip to Lebanon and was joined in East Beirut by Bob Lodwick. The meeting was called for consultation with local Presbyterian church leaders. I drove across the Green Line to spend a few days in East Beirut, where the meetings were held, giving me a chance to confer face-to-face with our church staff people from New York and Geneva. We would share information and perspectives as we planned future strategies.

A day or two before this meeting, I had received a phone call from Sis Levin, the wife of Jeremy Levin, Cable News Network executive, who had been kidnapped on March 7, 1984, two months before Ben. We had not been in touch before the call; in fact, we would laugh together later at our perception that the U.S. State Department seemed interested in keeping us apart. Sis had been told that I was not really a Christian, while my family members had been told that Sis was a little bit crazy.

Sis Levin was growing increasingly disturbed by the urging from the State Department and Cable News Network that she not say or do anything public. She made what she described as "a most an-

Ben: "How in the world did a Presbyterian missionary end up in such a situation?"

John and his mother: "I couldn't have managed without him."

Standing behind their parents, left to right, Chris, Ann, Sue, and John Weir: "The family looked just the way I remembered them."

Alvin Puryear, Ben, Fred Wilson, and Carol at Ben's first press conference: "The church was the right setting."

Father Martin and Ben, London, July 31, 1986: "A friend is waiting to see you."

Ben and Carol: "Called to look to the world and its needs."

guished decision." On October 23 she went on the *Today Show* to talk about her husband's kidnapping.

Now she was calling to say that she was on her way to Damascus. Would I like to join her? She felt sure we could make good progress by working together. She sounded optimistic and I was sorely tempted to go there again. However, the fall semester at the seminary had just begun. I thought it over and called her back, suggesting that she go on to Damascus and keep in touch with me. I could join her there by driving over the mountains in a few hours if something developed. As it turned out, the men were not released at that time. However, Sis was later credited, through her contact with officials in Damascus, with aiding in Jerry's release.

I was determined to visit Nabih Berri, Lebanese Minister of Justice and leader of Amal, and was quickly granted an appointment. It was easier to gain a face-to-face interview with an official in Lebanon than it was in Washington! This seemed strange to someone raised to believe that the United States was a government of the people, by the people, and for the people, but I did not feel the full sting of this realization until I carried my campaign for Ben's release to the United States a few months later.

Arpiné Hanna, a woman colleague and very good friend, agreed to go with me for this interview. Passing through the heavily guarded entrance, we waited briefly in a dimly lit reception room. The atmosphere outside was tense. New fighting had erupted just about the time we had set off by taxi. A young woman met us and ushered us into the minister's office. It was very small and Mr. Berri was sitting at his desk, phone in hand, seeking to deal with this new fighting. Another young man joined us. I suspected that he was a person with useful contacts among those who were holding Ben, but he didn't speak during our conversation.

Mr. Berri said that he knew of Ben and his activities for relief and assistance during the war years. He assured me that Ben was not kidnapped because of anything against him personally. It was clearly because of the general political climate.

He told me that he was against the kidnapping of Americans, but that his militia did not have power over Hezbollah, the group which he said held Ben. Mr. Berri said that the hostage group considered him too conciliatory, too pro-Western. They called him an American. However, he said that Ben was alive and well.

Mr. Berri startled me by saying that the U.S. government was doing nothing for Ben and the others. I had had the uneasy feeling from my own encounters with embassy people that this was the case. Mr. Berri said that perhaps after the November elections, the government might get serious about helping to free the hostages. Could

Amal free Ben? I asked. Mr. Berri said that the militia had worked on Ben's case. He had contacts who made inquiries once a week and continued to make every effort to free both Jeremy Levin and Ben. He himself worked with an intermediary. He claimed that he had been able to deliver a videotape to another party (unnamed) which proved that the men were alive. He also said that the kidnapping was related to the Shiite prisoners in Kuwait.

He named Syria as the key to release of the Americans. Syria was cooperative. They did not have complete control but were able to apply pressure. His deputy suggested that I write to President Assad. "Would press attention help?" No, he did not think that such use of the media would be useful. "You are a religious person. Pray," advised Mr. Berri.

As we left, the sound of artillery fire came from nearby. The taxi took a very roundabout route to get to our apartment in West Beirut. The streets were empty. The atmosphere bristled with tension. I thought about the interview and was thankful that at least Ben appeared to be still alive.

In November Fred Wilson received a call from the Rev. Wyatt Tee Walker, the Rev. Jesse Jackson's New York associate. A responsible leader of one of the militias in Lebanon wanted to know if the Rev. Jackson would be willing to go to Damascus to receive Ben Weir. According to this conversation, those holding Ben would release him, but not the other Americans.

On behalf of all the Americans, Jackson told this contact that they all deserved to be released. However, he said he would go to Syria even if only one was to be freed, especially a fellow clergyman. Rev. Walker would be contacted about arrangements around the tenth of December. It was expected that Ben, at least, would be freed in Damascus upon Rev. Jackson's arrival.

The Program Agency was informed of this conversation and agreed to sponsor the trip financially. If the process for Ben's release failed, the church would send a delegation to Damascus anyway to explore the release of all the hostages. The proposed trip would be made before Christmas. Because I was uncertain about the security of my telephone in Beirut, this whole episode was not immediately communicated to me.

My sense of urgency for Ben's release included my awareness of the broad political situation in the region. The chaotic war in Lebanon and the war between Iran and Iraq played an important role in the flow of other political decisions. Everything could change at a moment's notice. The shelling by the Israelis of Palestinians in Baalbek or in the camps on the outskirts of Beirut made me nervous. The

Palestinians and the political groups supporting them considered the actions of the Israelis as extensions of American policy. Relatives of the victims of these Israeli attacks had found shells bearing American manufacture marks near the bodies of loved ones and in the midst of destroyed homes.

The nightly sounds of battles across the Green Line in Beirut made me even more edgy and fearful for Ben. Was he being held in one of the places under attack? Would he be blamed for these "American"-supported attacks?

In late November a Lebanese political leader said to the Rev. Salim Sahiouny at a meeting in Beirut, "Your pastor is going to be released." Mr. Sahiouny reported this conversation to me with great excitement. Then, early in December on my way to school, I stopped at the grocery store next to the seminary. Had I heard? Peter Kilburn had disappeared. Conjecture was that he had been kidnapped. The grocer expressed great sadness. He knew Peter well, as did Ben and I. In fact, Peter and Ben had attended the same junior high school in Berkeley. I had stopped to chat with Peter just a few days before Ben was kidnapped. A stroke had left him partially paralyzed, and he walked with a cane. In addition, he needed medicine for his high blood pressure. If he had been kidnapped, what would be the state of his health?

On December 6 a most disturbing incident occurred in the Middle East: a Kuwaiti airplane was hijacked to Tehran. American officials believed that the skyjackers were Shiites, the same people accused of the earlier bombing of the U.S. Embassy and the marine barracks in Lebanon.

At least six Americans were aboard the plane, of whom three were officials of the U.S. Agency for International Development. Two of these AID officials were shot, and two American women were among those released and flown to Pakistan.

American intelligence officials said the skyjacking seemed to be part of a continuing effort by Hezbollah to gain the release of the seventeen prisoners held in Kuwait, convicted of bombing the American and French embassies in Kuwait exactly one year earlier. Could the hijackers be the same group holding Ben and the others?

On December 9, Iranian security forces stormed the skyjacked Kuwaiti airliner at the Tehran airport. They freed the last nine hostages and took the four hijackers into custody.

Once the incident was concluded, the press turned to other concerns. For those of us who had hoped to hear of Ben's release around this date, this hijacking was of special concern. Was there some connection between this tragedy and our own? The demands were the same. Fred Wilson contacted the Rev. Wyatt Tee Walker. Had he heard further from his source in Damascus about Ben's release? There was no word, no word at all.

Finally the message came. The time was not right. Neither Ben nor any of the others could be released. I suspected that the hijacking incident had destroyed any hope of goodwill by embarrassing both Kuwait and Iran. This was confirmed a few weeks later. Brutality and recrimination were expressed by all sides. Would there ever be a climate in which common sense could reign?

In any case, I had asked friends in Egypt to make reservations for Ben and for the rest of us. We would all gather to spend Christmas at the Anglican guest house in Zumalik, a suburb of Cairo.

On December 11 Sue arrived in Beirut to go with me to Cairo. Dear, faithful Sue. I drove to the airport to meet her. A political science major at the University of California, she was more conversant with international perspectives than the rest of us. She always had good ideas to offer and was the member of the family who stayed in close contact with the State Department.

Sue, much like Ben, has a great big heart and is always ready to be helpful. The airport was functioning in December of 1984 and the flight to Egypt was easy enough. John met us as we landed. How good it was to be getting together. At the guest house, Ann was waiting, filled with good humor. We were cordially welcomed and shown to our rooms. Chris arrived shortly. Sue's husband, John Nelson, came in around midnight on a delayed flight.

The next morning we were off by train to Aswan. The train was comfortable, a vast improvement over one Ben and I took in 1976. We bunched together and played word games as we looked forward to Christmas. In Aswan we had pleasant rooms facing the Nile. It was a joy to sit looking at the garden with its large bushes of poinsettias. The food was excellent, and we had more than enough to eat. The more I realized the beauty and joy of this trip, the harder it became for me. I kept remembering the earlier trip to this place with Ben. We had had such a fine time. Now we were here, but he was not.

That afternoon we explored the streets of Aswan. John and Ann picked out a silver lotus-shaped necklace for me which I was to wear for special remembrance in the coming months. We attended a candlelight service at a German mission hospital and sang Christmas songs in Arabic, German, and English.

The first night we sat up late talking together. Whenever we met after an absence we always did this. Each idea concerning Ben's kidnapping was analyzed from every possible angle. I was very grateful to the Presbyterian Church for making this visit possible. I loved these young people so much. They were filled with ideas and seemed to form a united source of power and energy. Although they were suffering themselves, they were totally supportive of me and thoroughly behind every effort we could make to gain Ben's freedom.

They decorated Ann and Christine's hotel room with Christmas stockings containing our pile of gifts. I had brought gifts purchased in Lebanon, Christine had toted gifts from Saudi Arabia, and the others offered presents from Egypt and California.

I thanked God for each member of our family, and we prayed for Ben, wherever he was, asking God to have him treated well and find some way to celebrate the birth of Christ. *Oh, God, please release him soon!* After Christmas in Aswan, we moved on by train to Luxor to celebrate New Year's Eve there. Upon our arrival we were handed a telex from President Reagan. He said that he knew we were missing Ben during the holiday season and that he and Nancy were praying for us. We appreciated this message, but we continued to hope that he would intercede personally on our behalf for the release of the hostages.

15

"I'm going to break your legs and arms!"

I was comfortably warm most of the time in my new room from the heat of the radiator, though there were days when the central heating system did not function. Two panes of glass were missing from the window near me, and two more on the other side of the room. When the cold wind blew, I felt it! I kept asking if I could have something to keep my head warm. In the clutter of one corner a guard found a dirty stocking cap someone had thrown away. They said I could wash it and use it. I did and it worked fine. With my blankets and my fleece-lined pajamas, gloves, and stocking cap I was reasonably comfortable. I was able to study my Arabic New Testament hour after hour without interruption or discomfort.

One day a new guard came into the room and noticed that I had been reading my little volume. He asked me what the book was. I said it was the *Injil*—the Gospel. He asked if he could borrow it and look at it. I said I was glad to share it with him but hoped he would bring it back. As he picked it up and thumbed through the pages, he noticed that the Gospel of Matthew came first and the Gospel of Mark was second. He said, "What is this? I thought that there was only one Gospel."

"Yes," I replied, "there are four Gospel stories. They make up one book." I told him to read the introduction and then look in the table of contents and observe how there are really four parts of the same Gospel. He took the New Testament and went away. After perhaps thirty minutes he came back into the room and handed me the New Testament. "This is not the true Gospel. There are four Gospels here. We know from the Koran that one Gospel came down from heaven. How can you say there are four?"

I said, "There is one story about the good news of God's mercy and grace, and this tells us how the good news came and was proclaimed by Christ. But four different persons wrote, under the inspiration of God, from four different angles. This is God's message for everyone."

This he could not accept. He maintained that the true Gospel had been lost, and what was now between the pages was not true. It had been changed. "We know," he said, "that Jesus was not really executed; Judas died in his place, deservedly, because he was not faithful. God rescued Jesus and took him up to heaven. He was a good man, and God would not allow him to be harmed."

I explained how God had allowed Jesus to suffer in order to show us how God is with us in our suffering, how in the midst of our pain he cares for us and saves us. I went on to say that it is true that Jesus was raised by the power of God from death and that he continues to be with God in heaven.

The guard was unwilling to consider any other interpretation, because he believed he knew the true story. He went out, closed the door, and never talked about the matter again. This was typical of my many conversations with Muslim believers over the years. There is a vast gulf of misunderstanding and a tremendous gap in our approach to the scriptures. I wished there were more opportunities to explore our different points of view and try to come to some resolution. This was only a brief interlude. It was disappointing that the opening for further discussion never came.

The next morning to my surprise, after breakfast, the guard brought me a jigsaw puzzle! It was still in its original wrapper and had over a thousand pieces. On the box was a picture of the completed puzzle.

To my great surprise it showed a scene familiar to me—the historic marketplace in front of the Grand Palace in Brussels, Belgium. Carol and I had visited there on our way back to Lebanon a year before, and it brought back many happy memories. As I opened the package and started putting the puzzle together, I realized that this was the first day of the New Year. I was really having a New Year's Day party. I spread the pieces out on the floor, but it was too much of a task for one day, so I spaced it out over a week.

It did not take me long to realize that my chain's length enabled me to open the window. I was not sure whether to take a chance on following my curiosity. I remembered the trouble I had gotten into in the past, but I decided to try to see what was out there early the next morning before the guards were awake, so I was up well before the first call to prayer. Very carefully and slowly I opened the window just a crack. To my surprise and delight I was looking westward out over the Bekaa Valley at the Lebanon Mountains on the other side. In the valley below I could see a streetlight here and there. I closed the outer shutter and inside window noiselessly and went back to sleep.

At daylight I was up again and looked out at the snow-covered mountains which could be seen so clearly. The first rays of the sun turned the entire range to pastel pink. I thought of it as my million-dollar view. I did not dare to look long, but closed the window with a fresh image of that beautiful scene still in my mind. Every morning I was up early to see this view. Soon I discovered that by looking to the extreme right I could see the ruins of the ancient Roman structures of the temple of Baalbek. I knew then that I was close to the city, only a few kilometers to the north. I could also see the major highway coming out of Baalbek and going south through the Bekaa Valley.

Later when I went to the bathroom I found that by standing on the toilet I could look out the window and see the same ruins in front of me. That sight, and the memory of it throughout the day, spoke to me of the grandeur of the Creator and his good intentions for the world and its people. This gave me hope and a sense of harmony.

One early morning in late January I made a serious mistake. I heard a loud voice yelling, "Close that window!" The guard was outside on the veranda and saw exactly what was happening. He came storming into the room in a rage and scolded me severely but did not beat me. He made monstrous threats before he went out, and I really thought my life was in danger. Soon he returned with a short length of chain. He chained my right wrist through the radiator and connected it with my right foot.

This meant that I could not use my right hand easily, nor could I stretch out to my full length on my mattress. I also could not get support for my back but was kept in a half-sitting posture. He made it clear that this was my punishment. It seemed mild compared to what I had imagined.

I remained in that uncomfortable posture for several days until the chain was removed and I was sternly told never to open the window again. So I kept the window closed; the risk of taking another look at the view was entirely too great. However, I found that by standing on my mattress and looking down through the shutters from a certain angle I could see the area immediately in front of the building. Occasionally a shepherd passed by with a herd of sheep on the way to or from a pasture on the rocky hillside. One time I saw children playing with a ball at a house some distance away; another time I saw a woman hanging up her family washing—all welcome diversions.

During these days there were often books to read, but nothing of great value. Most interesting was a book of poetry written by a German at the end of World War I, reflecting on his experiences of returning home and later wandering in the southern Bavarian Alps.

The book had been translated into English and published in America with some of his art sketches.

The murder mysteries occupied my time but were of little value. The worst book was the story of a huge fantastic snake that got out of its cage in California and terrorized a large area with its lethal bite. Finally the hero shot it. It was so impossible it was funny.

During the preceding seven months I had been reading and studying the Arabic New Testament carefully, continuing to find new messages in it as well as new questions I would want to study in the future.

Twice during the month of January the guard allowed me to see videotapes prepared in the United States. The selections were not much to my liking, but they did offer diversion for an hour or so. The effort to provide entertainment indicated that the captors were interested in keeping me—and probably other hostages—in a reasonable state of mind.

As I listened daily to footsteps back and forth to the bathroom in the morning, it seemed that there were four or possibly five others. I did not detect among them the woman I had heard earlier. Even with the diversion of a few books and two video shows, I continued to be very much by myself. I felt my isolation and distance from people I loved and yearned for the time when I would be free.

Finally St. Valentine's Day came. Remembering the parties our family had enjoyed over the years and recalling early childhood experiences on this happy day. I decided to try to celebrate by myself. But on the morning of February 14, I was aroused by the yell of a guard calling urgently to another guard. He was in a room at the end of a short hallway and was obviously excited. I could hear him throw open the window to the veranda as he waited for the other guard to join him. I had already decided that another hostage was being held in that room, because I had heard him talking to the guard in English. It was clear from the confusion that the hostage was not in the room any more. He had escaped! As soon as the second guard came, they undertook a careful search of the area.

Could the mysterious hostage get away safely? What would his escape mean to me? Perhaps he would be able to tell others where we were, which might aid in rescuing us. On the other hand, if his escape should lead to military action and an attempt to rescue us by force, this would only lead to our death.

Within an hour more guards had arrived. They seemed to take the matter very seriously. A man came into my room with a length of chain and proceeded to chain my one free hand and foot to the radiator again. Obviously he did not want to take any chance of a second hostage escaping.

That evening there was fresh activity in the apartment, and before the night had gone very far I was unchained, led out of the apartment, taken downstairs, and thrust roughly into a car. We drove a very short distance and then I was taken out again and led into some underground space. I heard an iron door being opened. I was led inside, and the door was closed and padlocked.

I was in an underground cell with a bed, a bowl, a spoon, and a light bulb overhead. This setting aroused my suspicion and anxiety, wondering what might now take place. My cell was dark and cramped compared to the room I had been in. In the move my New Testament had been left behind.

After perhaps an hour or so I heard the door being unlocked. I was led out to a small vehicle and told to lie down. I found myself in a narrow space that appeared to be behind the front seat of an enclosed jeep. The vehicle started out and bounced along very rough roads. I could hear rain and sleet driving against the metal roof.

The driver was having a hard time getting the vehicle over the unimproved roads. The trip was up and down so that I very quickly lost a sense of direction. I could tell later that we were riding over a smooth surface. At the end of forty-five minutes or more, we stopped. I was taken out and was led with very great caution into a building and upstairs. There I was told that I must sit down and remain very quiet. I could feel that there was a warm stove in the room.

I could also sense the presence of other people. Someone coughed quietly. The sound of a guard whispering to another guard could be heard from time to time. In a few minutes I was given a cup of tea and a piece of bread. After consuming this snack, I was told to lie down and go to sleep on the floor. There was a rug on the floor and I was given a very thin cushion for my head. During the night I awakened and took the risk of peeking to see where I was. I could see other sleeping forms and could tell that I was in a family apartment in a small living room crowded with furniture. I remembered that I had heard one guard say to another, "My wife is away." Apparently he had arranged this as a temporary stopping place for us all. In the morning I was taken to a bathroom that contained a small washing machine. This confirmed my impression that I was staying in a family's modest apartment.

We were moved again the following night. I was driven a very short distance by car and taken into a cold building, where I was told to lie down on a thin air mattress and go to sleep. Later I heard the guards get up for early morning prayer and then go back to sleep. Once I was sure they were sound asleep I took a chance and peeked to see where I was. I found myself in a large room with the guards sleeping at one end. Paper covered the windows, and the room seemed quite bare.

Later the guards brought in large sheets of pressed fiberboard and pieces of lumber, which they took into the adjoining room. Soon they were sawing and hammering, making places for us.

When the noise stopped, I understood that the guards had begun taking the hostages, one by one, to the next room. Eventually I was taken there too and told to lie down on a mattress. Once again I was chained to the wall. As soon as the door was closed I looked around at my new home. I found myself in a stall. On one side, a hastily constructed partition of pressed wood extended a few feet beyond my mattress. At my head and along the other side of the mattress was a wall. It was wet. The concrete ceiling was about eight feet above my head. Apparently a series of stalls had been created for several hostages. This proved to be the most dismal environment of my entire captivity.

When the guard was not looking, I peeled back a small piece of the paper on the window and looked out. The ground was covered with a very heavy frost. Not far away there were several one-story houses. Parked near them was a large tank truck and two cars. We had been moved to a small village on a gradually sloping hillside and were in a workshop or storage building.

The guards were extremely quiet and demanded that I remain silent too. They did not even allow me to cough or clear my throat. Sometimes I could hear children outside. At these times, the guards would stand next to me and insist I be quiet.

The bathroom was the kind one would expect to find in a mechanic's garage. In one corner there was a simple hole in the floor. The other corner had a washbasin with a cold-water tap. An electric meter was on one wall.

In the afternoon, when the door to the guards' room was closed, I tried to make contact with whoever was in the stall next to me. Through a crack in the overlapping fiberboard, I whispered, "My name is Ben Weir, a Protestant pastor. Who are you?"

A whispered answer came back: "Lawrence Martin Jenco, Catholic priest."

Wow! A fellow human being close by, and a Christian leader as well. Without further communication, I felt his closeness and support and began praying for him.

Later I heard voices in the guards' room and assumed some additional member of their group had entered. After a while the door opened, and I felt someone come and sit on my mattress close to me. In a low voice, he whispered in Arabic in my ear, "I want you to write a letter. I will tell you in Arabic what to say, and you put it in your own words."

He had me sit so I could not see him but could write. First he read his statement straight through and then repeated the main ideas. He told me to address it to my church's top authorities. I dated it February 15, 1985, and addressed it to Dr. William P. Thompson, Stated Clerk. Then I copied it and addressed it to Dr. J. Oscar McCloud, General Director of the Program Agency. In the letter I urged effective action by the U.S. government to bring about release of prisoners held in Kuwait. I also stressed that my captors rejected any third-party attempts at intervention.

When I had finished, the stranger asked me to translate into Arabic what I had written. He seemed satisfied, took the papers and ball-point pen, and left. I wondered what would be the outcome. At least this was an attempt at communication, and that was a sign of hope. But I was skeptical that Kuwait would be flexible on the issue, or that the U.S. government would bend.

Later that day the same man (so I supposed) returned. He whispered to the person in the stall next to mine. Then he came to me, saying, "Here is *Abuna* [Father] Jenco. Tell him to write the same kind of letter."

I told my new hostage acquaintance what he was to do. I repeated the same instructions I had received, including the fact that he would need to write carefully, since he would be given only two small sheets of paper for identical copies of his text. I translated again from the Arabic and summarized the main ideas. There was strict control and no opportunity for us to converse. Once finished, Father Jenco moved back to his stall and the stranger departed. Again, I wondered skeptically about any positive outcome but was encouraged by the attempt to do something on our behalf.

The two guards prepared our simple meals in the large room, which was between the bathroom and the hostages' quarters. They seemed to stay near the windows. They kept a radio on very low volume. I had the impression that they were constantly on the look-out to see if anyone was approaching. On our second or third day there was an increase of activity on the inside and outside of the building. The next time I went to the bathroom I noticed that an electric circuit breaker had been added. There were large wires leading to it but not engaged. On this same day one of the guards said to me, "It is extremely important to be quiet all the time. The building is now 'loaded.' If there is an attempt to rescue you by Syrians or Americans or others, we are prepared to set off the explosives with you and us inside it." I went to sleep that night wondering what I could do to prevent this eventuality.

The next morning I awoke with the memory that the building was armed with explosives. I waited for several hours to be taken to the bathroom, but no guard appeared as had been the case here for the previous days. I could hear whimpering puppies nearby. It seemed to me that they were in the room where the guards stayed. I began turning over in my mind why there was no evidence of the presence of the guards and why the puppies seemed to be in the next room.

As time went on the idea occurred to me that the guards had left the building, but had put the dogs in their place. Perhaps this was a trick to get someone from the village to attempt to get into the building. Anyone trying to get in would blow the structure up with us in it. The guards themselves would be safe. Could this be a fiendish plot to execute the hostages? I could not be sure that my thinking was right, but the idea more and more impressed itself on me. By now I badly needed to go to the bathroom but knew I had to think this through calmly.

In desperation I took my empty drinking bottle and urinated into it. Now I could think more clearly. I took the risk of crawling to the end of my mattress and peered around the partition. I saw another man with a beard. In short whispers I asked who he was. I learned that he was Father Martin Jenco. "I am Ben Weir. Where are the guards?"

He didn't know anything about them. I told him I feared that the building was prepared for destruction and we had to prevent having it blown up. He motioned that he had no suggestions.

I heard another voice in a distant stall say, "I am Buckley . . . William Buckley. Who are you?"

Still whispering, I replied, "Ben Weir."

I decided to take the desperate action of calling for help. If I could attract someone's attention, I could warn him that he should not enter the building but go for help. Maybe in the absence of guards someone with experience could come, disarm the building, and free us.

I peeled back the paper from the window and opened it. No one was near the building. There was snow on the ground. I could see, in the distance, two men trying to get a car started. I called in Arabic, *"Ya muallim, saaidna!"* ("Oh, sir, help us!"). One of the men in the distance stopped for a minute. Then he went right on with his task of starting the car. My efforts were hopeless.

At that moment the inside door to the guards' room opened and a guard stood in the doorway. He looked dazed, as if he had just awakened from a very deep sleep. I realized that my speculations were all wrong! He was extremely angry and came charging at me like a bull. I pulled down my mask quickly to avoid seeing him. I heard him slam the window and lock it.

Then he proceeded to beat me and stomp on me, saying over and over, "I'm going to break your legs and arms!" After giving vent to his wrath, he said, "Now I'm going to show you!"

He went back into his room and then returned, apparently without a weapon. He ordered me to lie face down on the mattress and put my hands behind my back. He then taped my hands together with thick plastic tape. He had me turn over and lie on my hands while he chained me by my feet. Then he went out.

Soon he came back, still fuming. "Do you know what I could do to you? I could put TNT in your jacket pockets, set you outside, and let you blow yourself up. That would serve you right." Still in a stew, he went back into his room, closing the door with a curse.

All during that day I learned how uncomfortable it is to lie on one's hands. Occasionally I would sit up briefly to relieve some of the pressure—my hands and shoulders were becoming very sore and painful—but I was not able to maintain that position very long. Throughout the day I was given no water or food, and I understood this to be my punishment for doing a forbidden act. It was Sunday, and I trusted other people were praying for me. I needed their prayers.

At nightfall, after the other hostages had been fed, a guard came and talked with me. He wanted to know what had happened. I explained the situation exactly as I had viewed it: I thought we had been left alone and that the building was going to blow up. He was surprised at this reaction and went to great pains to explain that although the building was prepared for demolition, under no circumstances would the guards ever leave. They were prepared to be martyrs if the building had to be destroyed. He told me, very seriously, that I had narrowly escaped being executed and if I did anything in future that was suspect, my life would be in peril.

I assured him I did not want this to happen and he could expect me to cooperate. I was then given food and water. However, after I had eaten, new chains were brought and I was shackled with my two feet together and my two hands together. My hands were connected to my feet, so that I couldn't straighten out. I could assume a sitting position but without any possibility of finding support for my back against the wall.

This remained my condition for several days. The chains were taken off only each morning during the time I was taken to the bathroom. However, I found I could go to sleep at night and managed somehow to get blankets over me to keep warm. The room was damp, the walls were moist, and the ceiling was continually covered with droplets of water. When someone walked outside, I could hear the crunching of snow.

At this same time the water supply failed. The guards said that the pipes had frozen. However, I heard the guards talking among themselves about how the water company had cut off the supply of water that was supposed to come into the building. This meant that once a day a guard surreptitiously brought a container of water to the building for the use of all of us. I assumed that there were four hostages and two guards. There seemed to be very little water to meet our needs. In the morning there was a four-ounce glass of tea with breakfast. In the afternoon there would be a stew which had juice with it, and in the evening a sandwich with four ounces of water. In addition there might be half a bottle of water from time to time. There were no bottles for collecting urine, but small tin cans were provided for that purpose.

During the coldest days a guard would bring into the room a container of bottled gas attached to a heater. There would be heat for an hour or more, which would partially dry off a spot on the ceiling. The effect did not last long. In the humid atmosphere everything seemed to be damp and clammy. I could tell that Father Martin in the stall next to me was feeling the cold even more than I. I prayed for him, and I knew that he was praying for me.

It became apparent that the guards did not like the environment of the cramped rooms any more than I did. Almost daily they would say in one way or another, "We are going to move to a better location where there will be warmth and dryness. It will be comfortable and you will like it."

After a few days while I was still chained hand and foot I could tell from the sounds that guards had come to unlock Father Martin and take him into the other room. It seemed that each hostage was taken from the stalls into the other room. I was then unchained and moved into the stall where Father Martin had been. On the wall was a faintly drawn cross, a new call to devotion. Once again I was chained hand and foot. I found the chains very restrictive. I did whatever I could to exercise in some way, even in some partial way. When I thought the guards were not likely to come into the room, I managed to get into a squatting position to exercise my legs as much as possible. I would lie on my back and arch my back. I would also move my arms. I thought it was important to maintain muscle tone.

Eventually, I was chained by only one foot and one hand, and I was once again able to enjoy the luxury of back support when I sat up.

It became apparent that the guards also hoped for a change. Finally, one night about ten days after Father Martin had been moved, I was blindfolded, taken by car a very short distance into another building, and placed in a new stall for a further three months.

16

"Have you been to Washington?"

Following our Christmas holiday in Cairo, I returned directly to Beirut, only to travel the next day to the United States. I needed to confer with Fred Wilson and the other staff members of the Presbyterian Church. I was becoming more and more restless. Several times I had thought that Ben was about to be released, and nothing had happened. The political situation in Beirut was so unpredictable.

When I arrived in New York on January 5, I had a brief meeting with Rev. Jesse Jackson at Kennedy Airport on his return from a trip to Europe. He said he would continue to work for the release of the hostages. I hoped he would be successful. I knew he had already demonstrated skill in communicating with people of the Middle East, and we appreciated his support.

I also appeared with Sis Levin on the *Today Show*. John Palmer was generous and supportive as he interviewed us. Sis was very articulate, as she pressed for more action for the release of the hostages and the need to work for peace. We had a friendly breakfast together after the show. We both felt we had given the "quiet diplomacy" of the State Department more than enough time to work. It was now time to make the public aware of the hostage issue.

If the State Department had decided not to act further for the hostages' release, what were we to do? Ben and I had pledged our commitment to one another in the sight of God. Wasn't this a matter of better or worse, life or death? Sis and I parted with the determination to be in closer touch with each other. We would goad our government into action on behalf of its citizens every way we could.

While still in New York City on January 8, I read the story of the fifth American to be kidnapped from the streets of Beirut since last March, a Roman Catholic priest, Father Lawrence Martin Jenco, who had been working with Catholic Relief Services. This agency serves people suffering in Lebanon, providing relief and rehabilitation projects all over the country. Father Martin had been grabbed from his car very near our home in West Beirut. A Servite priest, he had been in Beirut only since September.

In late January, I was back in Beirut when I heard that hostage William Buckley had been seen in a videotape that was broadcast in the States, standing against a blank wall, holding a newspaper, and saying, "Today is the twenty-second of January, 1985. I am well and my friends Benjamin Weir and Jeremy Levin are also well. We ask that our government take action for our release quickly."

Once again, the State Department response was the same: "We honestly don't know for sure who we are dealing with or where the prisoners are or what we are supposed to do to get them released." And when President Reagan was asked by reporters what the United States was doing to obtain the prisoners' release, he said, "That's something we can't talk about. But believe me, this is very much in our minds. We haven't forgotten that they're in captivity. I don't think it would be productive for us to talk about what we're doing."

Asked if the efforts were making progress, Mr. Reagan replied, "I'm not going to tell the score." Quiet diplomacy!

Early in February, John and Sue went to a meeting at Jackson's Chicago headquarters of Operation PUSH. Buckley's plea for quick government action had been aired on the networks. There were about 200 people present. On the platform with John, Sue, Sis Levin, and members of the Jenco family was a Muslim dignitary who offered a prayer in Arabic. Jesse Jackson had recently returned from his trip to Europe, where he had made contact with people he thought would be helpful. He was tired but upbeat on the issue of the hostages.

Sis Levin had arranged for John to be on the syndicated *Kup's Show* on Chicago television. This weekend included many firsts for John and Sue: first talk show for our son, first meeting with Jesse Jackson, first press conference, and first meeting with other hostage families.

Ann came to Beirut to be with me in early February between semesters at her school. It had rained the day before, and I drove to the airport past huge pools of water in the streets. As we left the airport, several fast-moving cars full of young men waving guns out the windows raced down the roadway. Drivers were pulling over to the side of the road to let them pass. We wondered who they were chasing as they gunned past us.

Ann was silent for a few moments. "Mother, the family thinks you should leave Lebanon as soon as possible. There are too many dangers here. The anarchy and lawlessness can only bring trouble for you. I don't want to visit Beirut again under these conditions." I knew she was right. We hurried into town, glad to reach our apartment house safely.

I didn't like to have Ann out in the streets alone. We walked almost everywhere together. She visited old school friends and was great company for me. I was sorry to see her leave.

As I walked into the seminary on my way to class on February 14, a reporter stopped me and told me that hostage Jeremy Levin, bureau chief for Cable News Network, had been freed after being held for eleven months. She wanted my opinion. I was still not used to dealing with reporters. I replied that I really didn't know very much about it but that I was, of course, delighted that he was free and hoped the other men would be released soon.

Late that afternoon Arpiné and I went to the offices of NBC. Perhaps we could learn something more. We saw the tape made of Jeremy, bearded and looking very tired. He had arrived at a Syrian checkpoint in the Bekaa Valley, was received by the Syrians, and was to be released shortly to the U.S. Ambassador in Damascus.

We were filled with a mixture of disappointment, despair, and hope. If Jeremy had been released, why not Ben? At the same time, Jeremy's freedom gave us some hope that somehow Ben too might be freed.

The next day an article in the *New York Times* indicated that according to the Administration the Syrians had played a positive and much-appreciated role in Jeremy's release. *USA Today* reported that Jeremy said he had been asked by the President not to discuss any details about the others being held.

The official Syrian press agency reported that their foreign minister had told the U.S. Ambassador to Syria that Mr. Levin had managed to escape. Earlier in the day the Syrian Ambassador in Washington said his government won Mr. Levin's release through negotiations. Jeremy was quoted as saying that he fled from his captors and walked for two hours until he came across a Syrian checkpoint. The next day I read in the *Daily Star,* the English-language newspaper in Beirut, that Islamic Jihad had freed Jeremy Levin through the mediation of a prominent Muslim. The article also stated that an investigation had determined that he had not been involved in any espionage against Islamic forces. I was greatly disturbed by an added note indicating that Islamic Jihad did indeed have the other Americans, they were to be brought to trial as spies, and one was to be executed.

In the meantime I heard on the radio that Muhammad Ali was coming to Beirut to try to gain the release of the hostages. Perhaps his fame as former world heavyweight champion and his influence as an American Muslim would win their freedom. (When a crowd gathered outside a prominent Shiite mosque to greet him, clenching their fists and shouting in Arabic, "Death to Americans!" Ali, who doesn't understand Arabic, clenched his own fist in a well-intentioned show of solidarity.)

I met with Ali at his hotel. He greeted me warmly and we touched each other cheek-to-cheek, as is the custom in the Middle East. In a gentle voice, he said that he himself would someday meet his maker in Paradise, and he wanted to do something good. He wanted the whole world to turn to Islam, but because Americans were being kidnapped by Muslims, Islam was getting a bad name in the West. He had made a broadcast appealing to the captors to release those men they had threatened to kill. Killing was against the teaching of the Koran. I thanked him for coming to Lebanon and wished him success in his efforts. However, there was no change as a result of Ali's intercession.

I could not forget the newspaper report that quoted Islamic Jihad as saying its American hostages were going to be brought to trial and one of them would be executed. As I told Fred and Oscar by telephone, I thought Ben would either be released or killed. They were startled by the despair and discouragement in my voice, and the following day Fred called to say that Peggy Thomas would meet me in Beirut and go to Damascus with me. Alvin Puryear, Vic Jameson, Fred Wilson, and John would meet us there. If the Syrians had helped in Jeremy's release, perhaps they would be able to help Ben too.

Two days later Arpiné and I met Peggy at the Beirut airport. My plan was to go to Damascus and stay there until Ben was released. I would then return to Beirut to make arrangements for our apartment and seminary classes. Then I would leave for vacation with Ben. I was so optimistic that I packed a suitcase for him. If by any chance Ben was not released, I would return to Beirut after my two-week visa expired and continue to see what I could do on the local scene.

On February 21 I received a call from a member of the Shiite community whom I had known for a long time. She asked if I could visit her; there was something she had to tell me. I told her I was leaving the next day for Damascus. She said in that case she needed to see me that very night.

I reminded her that the streets were without lights and very dangerous. I was reluctant to go out alone. She replied, "I have a car and driver. I will come to see you."

No electricity. This meant no light on the streets, no light in the hall, no light on the stairwell. There was not even a doorbell to ring.

I told her I would take a flashlight and meet her at the bottom of the stairs.

She arrived promptly but would not come up to the apartment. We got into the back seat of her car and whispered together. We did not want our conversation overheard by the driver.

She said that she and her husband had been greatly distressed that Jeremy Levin had been released instead of their friend Ben Weir. They would use their influence in the Shiite community. Perhaps a prisoner exchange could be arranged. She said that her husband would be going to Damascus soon. He would meet me there at the Sheraton Hotel. How pleased I was to hear from this good friend. I knew that most of the Shiite community did not condone kidnapping. Many of them knew Ben personally and respected him and his work. I was greatly encouraged.

The next day Peggy Thomas and I were to drive to Damascus. The weather was problematic. It had rained steadily for several days—that meant snow in the mountains. But the driver of the car was confident that we could get through. We listened to the radio for news of the roads.

Early Thursday morning, February 21, we left the apartment bundled up for cold weather. We would be going through Druze territory, but the driver was Druze and well known by people who worked along this route, so we encountered no problems. Up in the mountains, however, the snow was heavy. We had no chains on the car. We were told the road was difficult. Snowplows had not been able to clear it. The driver turned to me. "I think we can make it. What do you think?"

I said, "Well, you know the road. If you think we can make it, go ahead."

We drove on slowly. Most of the other cars were turning back, but our driver spotted a friend of his who was stopped just ahead and pulled up alongside. They conferred. Yes, together the two cars might make it through.

After we had driven another mile or two on the slippery, snowy road, we were stopped at a roadblock. A Syrian soldier asked where we were going. I heard him say to the driver in Arabic, "If you want to die, go ahead; otherwise turn around."

The driver looked at me. "Let's turn around," I said. "I'm not yet ready to die." Apparently several trucks ahead of us had skidded off the road. It was now snowing very heavily. We went back to Beirut.

The next day we tried again and arrived in Damascus in good order. We breathed a sigh of relief as we met the others in the lobby of the Sheraton.

Fred and John arrived after stopping in London to see Terry

Waite. In January Terry had been instrumental in freeing British citizens held in Libya. Could he now be available to help us? Terry indicated that he had a backlog of work and travel with the Archbishop, but he would try to free his schedule as soon as possible.

This was the first time I had met Dr. Alvin Puryear. He was not a staff person of the church but the president of the Program Agency Board, which was responsible for Presbyterian workers overseas. We greeted each other a bit shyly but I welcomed and appreciated his presence. Already busy with his duties as Professor of Management at the City University of New York and consultant to a number of corporations, he volunteered his time to assume church responsibilities as well. I had not met Vic Jameson before either. As a writer and editor of *Presbyterian Survey* magazine, he was to prove an important resource in getting Ben's story out to the public.

The denomination had called for a cycle of prayer for the time we would be conferring in Damascus. Staff people would be supporting us with their prayers and love, beginning on Friday, February 22, and continuing until noon on February 28, focusing on the pastoral needs of Ben and our family and the success of our efforts in Damascus. Yet our people were called to include all people who were being held captive in the world and also those who were their captors.

The day we arrived, a telephone call came from the U.S. Embassy. Deputy Chief of Mission April Glaspie would like to have us as guests for lunch the next day, and the ambassador was inviting us to dinner. I thanked the caller but said to him, in a tone I hoped did not sound ungrateful, "But I have come for serious conversation. I hope we will have a chance to have such a discussion with Ambassador Eagleton." I hadn't been able to talk face-to-face with embassy personnel in Lebanon for quite a while and had had no word from them for weeks. It seemed easier to get down to business with our government here in Damascus.

The next day we all assembled in April Glaspie's home and engaged in small talk. Ambassador Eagleton came in and sat down with us for a few minutes before we went in to lunch. He was not free to stay, but he welcomed us to his home that evening.

I was getting a little uptight. My husband's life was at stake. When were we going to get down to business? These social gatherings avoided real work on the problem. When the ambassador got up to leave, I walked out with him to the hall entranceway. I was direct. "Mr. Ambassador, I have waited many months for our diplomatic effort to work. What exactly is our government doing for Ben's release?" He said that every day he went to the office of the Syrian foreign minister a few blocks away to press for the release of the hostages. I responded, "I expect to see the Syrians while I'm here, and then I'll find out what they are doing. What I want to know is, what is *our* government doing?"

"Well, have you been to Washington?" he asked.

His response hit me with surprising force. It also was to give me a whole new direction. I had to admit that I had not. Ambassador Eagleton was telling me that their staff did not know much, nor were they really doing anything. Their orders came from Washington.

At lunch I pressed the matter of the release of the seventeen prisoners in Kuwait. April Glaspie responded in an angry tone that this was not the issue. The embassy in Lebanon had shown us a videotape in which Ben read a statement that included this demand. Yet the Kuwaiti issue was downplayed.

That night, before dinner, Ambassador Eagleton and I spent about thirty minutes in discussion together. His chief concern was to stress that Jerry Levin had escaped. I needed to be convinced. The Syrian Ambassador in Washington had said that the Syrians had had a part in his release. Even the Reagan Administration had thanked the Syrians for their help. If Jerry Levin had escaped, I believed he was helped to do so.

Next day our group—which I began to refer to as a think tank—exchanged ideas. We knew that during the Israeli invasion into southern Lebanon in 1982, Iran had sent several hundred Iranian Revolutionary Guards through Syria into Lebanon, to be stationed in Baalbek in the eastern Bekaa Valley. Most of the rumors concerning the whereabouts of the hostages inside Lebanon centered on the Bekaa Valley, a stronghold of Lebanese Shiites who were inspired by the successful revolution in Iran. It did seem likely that Ben was being held in the Bekaa Valley. If the Syrians permitted Iranian Revolutionary Guards to be posted in their territory or travel through it, perhaps it would be helpful to talk with Iranian officials in Damascus.

The Iranian Ambassador to Syria was Ali Akbar Mushtashimi. About three months after the bombing of the marine headquarters in Beirut, he had received a package in the mail. The package detonated and the ambassador was wounded; one of his hands was blown off. As far as I knew, no one ever claimed responsibility for the bomb. The ambassador seemed to believe it had been sent by the CIA. When we asked if it would be possible to see him, we were told he had strong feelings against Americans and would not meet with them. In fact, he had been known to leave the room when an American entered.

We pressed for an appointment with Ambassador Eagleton in his office and finally met with him Monday at the embassy. Now, down to business. I did quite a bit of talking about Ben's situation. Why couldn't we get an appointment with Secretary of State George Shultz? We hoped the ambassador could help us.

Alvin Puryear was excellent at analyzing the dynamics of our meetings. He said little but observed much. It was he who pressed me to return to the States.

I hated to go. It seemed as if I were leaving Ben behind. I didn't know anything about Washington. What would I do or say there? If I stayed away very long, our apartment in Beirut would probably be occupied. There was also my teaching at the seminary. However, I was outvoted. The group was right. I would go to New York. Perhaps I could gain access to the Secretary of State.

After the others left, John and I remained for a few days, still trying unsuccessfully to see President Assad. (All we managed was an unproductive half hour with the Foreign Minister.) Back at the hotel, I telephoned the family of my Lebanese friend who had come at night in Beirut with an offer of help. Wonder of wonders, I was connected and talked with my friend's husband whom I had not been able to locate here in Damascus. Had something gone wrong? He assured me that everything would go all right and not to worry, and I had to be content with these vague but encouraging words.

On the twenty-third of February, during our stay in Damascus, Jeremy Levin returned to the United States and telephoned Sue. He said that as far as he knew he had always been held in the Baalbek area. He knew there had been others in the same building with him, but he did not know who they were. At one point, he had heard someone say in English, "Come." This would seem to indicate that they were Americans.

In January he said that his chains were removed before breakfast and he was able to move around the room and exercise. He also was given news of his wife and knew that she had been to Damascus. At Christmas he was given a pen and a Christmas card. He said that he never saw the faces of his captors. When he was moved, it was in a box lowered into the tank of a water truck. They always blindfolded and gagged him. He told Sue that he had tried to escape three times, tearing up pieces of sheet. Once when these pieces had been observed, he was in no way punished for it. The concern of the guards was for those prisoners held in Kuwait, and a number of times threats were made against his life.

I was getting very discouraged. Finally, as our visas would run out soon, John and I left a note of thanks for the President of Syria to be delivered by our embassy and prepared to leave.

The night before our departure, a call came around midnight from a news service in the United States: the Jenco family had received a letter from Father Martin. The voice at the other end of the phone line wanted to know if I had received a letter from Ben. No, I had not.

Why did the Jencos receive a letter and I didn't? We called Fred in New York, and he said that in fact the church staff had just received two letters. Since we were arriving in New York the next day, he wanted to meet us at the plane and put the letters in our hands.

John and I returned to the States on March 6. True to his word, Fred was waiting for us at the airport. He handed me two letters:

February 15, 1985

Dear Dr. McCloud,

I am writing to ask you to do everything in your means to demand that the U.S. government intervene effectively with the government of Kuwait because I understand that the U.S. government is not in fact acting effectively to secure the release of prisoners being held there. I am assured that once those prisoners are set free I and others will be released at the same time. This requires direct and effective action by the U.S. government with the government of Kuwait.

The men who hold me insist that they will refuse mediation or interference by any third party. They are opposed to Syria and will not deal with them, or any other party. If such interference is attempted I am told that our lives are in extreme danger and that the place where we are held will be blown up with us. So please ask the U.S. government to take this matter seriously.

Sincerely yours,

Benjamin M. Weir

The second letter was identical, except for being addressed to the previous Stated Clerk of the General Assembly, Dr. William P. Thompson. They had been sent from Beirut. The date of their delivery in New York was February 27. The letters were certainly in Ben's handwriting.

If I needed any incentive to go to Washington, there it was. Our work on Ben's behalf was more necessary than ever. He was reaching out to us for help. The demands of the captors were clearly impossible to meet without the intercession of the U.S. government.

17

*"If I survived this once,
I can do it again."*

I found myself in a narrow stall much like the one I had inhabited during February. This time the walls were gray and the ceiling higher. There was a hastily built partition on one side. On the other side was the wall and corner of the room. At the foot of my mattress two lengths of draped material hanging from a board overhead closed off the cubicle. The material was lightweight and I could see through it. I was back in a prison cell, but I could get some idea of what was taking place outside.

When the guard returned later on, I said to him, "I was moved so quickly that I did not have a chance to bring my Arabic New Testament. Will you please see if you can find it for me?" He promised that he would look for it. I repeated this request daily, but I never saw it again.

It soon became clear that my stall was located in a large, unfinished building. It seemed as if the structure was being renovated. There were no floor tiles. I was told one day to be sure to keep my ski mask on because the guards were working on the building. They seemed to be focusing on the ceiling.

When they had left, I looked at the ceiling above me and saw a frightening sight. There was a large plastic bag with two wires leading to it. This construction was hanging over my head. It was a plastic explosive charge! The wires must lead to a detonator. This was not a comforting thought. I would certainly be killed if or when it was exploded.

When I was taken to the bathroom, I found that a simple squat kind of toilet bowl had been set on the unfinished floor and a drainpipe introduced to the outside. There was a water spigot coming through the wall at which I could stoop and wash. This was the sum total of the bathroom facilities. This was where I also had to wash my plate, spoon, and cup.

When the guard was absent I could see that he had a mattress in the same room just a few steps from my cubicle. There was a table on the other side of the partition where he cooked the meals. At first the weather was comfortable, but as the weeks of spring went by, it got quite hot. This change of season also brought with it very large horseflies and ants. The guard brought a large can of insect repellent to keep the flies at bay. He usually sprayed morning and evening. In between, the flies would return.

Once in a while, a second guard would come into the room to talk with the first one. Apparently, the second guard lived in the building with his family and was creating the impression for relatives and neighbors that this room was rented to our guard as his own private residence. All this seemed to be intentional camouflage of the fact that hostages were held there. I was aware of another Arabic-speaking hostage in a far corner of the large room, out of sight behind a partition and curtains.

The first guard was very alert and anxious that there be no noise to give away our presence to outsiders. Frequently he looked out of the curtained windows to see who might be approaching the building. Eventually the guard secured a television set and would watch it or listen to his radio, but with the sound faintly audible. I could not see the TV, nor could I hear the radio distinctly. Occasionally I could catch phrases from some of the programs, but there was no news.

The radio programs that the guard listened to were apparently from a very conservative Shiite station in Lebanon. Occasionally there were broadcasts that explained the history of the Shiite people, what they believed, and how they interpreted the Koran. I was particularly interested in these interpretive programs. I wanted to learn as much as possible about the ultraconservative branch of this community and its history.

The guard himself was uncommunicative and at best had only a few words to say at mealtime. These three months were among the loneliest periods of my captivity. Like May and June 1984, once again I had no external resources and could rely only on my recent reading of the New Testament as well as passages memorized from the Old Testament. But I continued to find a great sense of purpose in intercessory prayer for people I knew in Lebanon, Syria, and other countries. I also continued to expect that eventually God would bring about my deliverance.

At the end of two months the guard was changed. A younger and less experienced man was put in charge. He was much more communicative and solicitous. The few times I could make out his form through the curtains, I saw that he wore glasses. The previous guard had refused to do anything to clean up the room, but the new guard proceeded to sweep regularly and keep the place in order. The previous guard refused to provide Kleenex, but my present captor was willing to do so. I no longer had to save tissues, dry them out, and use them a second time. During this time I developed a cough and ran a slight fever for a week. I concluded that I had a virus. Eventually it disappeared. I was thankful it was the only illness I had.

On April 10 I heard several men come into the building and go to a distant back room, from where I heard muffled male voices. After a long time, toward midday, several men entered my room and began to move some objects. Then one of them came to my cubicle, unlocked my chain, and led me out to stand against a wall. My mask was removed for a flash picture taken by a masked photographer and then replaced.

The guard took me back to my cubicle and gave me a notebook and a ballpoint pen, saying I could write a brief note to my wife and another to my family, but to use only one folded sheet from the copybook. He then proceeded to tell me what to write on the page to my wife. I was to acknowledge two messages that had come from her (he did not have them with him but would send them to me). Then he dictated in Arabic the remaining content: Men were held in Kuwait because they opposed U.S. policy supporting Israel. My wife should put pressure on the U.S. government for their release, knowing that upon their safety and freedom depended my own and that this was a difficult situation for me. (In the hasty writing I tried to blunt this sense of pressure for Carol.)

The guard was in a hurry and would allow me only a few brief moments to scratch a very short personal note to my family. I wrote this post-Easter greeting hastily, with tears in my eyes, assuring them of my hope and affection.

Once more I wondered what might be the effect of these messages and picture. At least they were a sign of new effort. Somehow God was at work.

May 8, 1985, came, the first anniversary of my capture. I heard the guard's footsteps walking toward my cubicle. To my surprise, he ordered me to turn away from him and remove my ski mask. Then he had me sit on a cement block. "I'm going to clean off this hair," he told me. Good, I thought, I'm going to have a haircut.

I needed it. The weather had turned hot. After a year my hair was down to my shoulders and my beard reached my chest. I would be cooler and cleaner now. However, when the guard started to use his clippers on my beard, it felt as if I were losing part of myself. I hadn't realized that the beard had become part of my self-image. My second surprise came when the guard handed me a piece of mirror to view the results. He had used the clippers on my head too. I looked like the traditional convict in the Middle East, where it is the custom to shave prisoners clean. I felt indignant at having joined the world's prison population. I was now the prisoner Everyman. But I knew that there were thousands of people in the world who were prisoners because of injustice. People are tortured and deprived for no reason other than that they are different. I was proud to be a prisoner for the Lord.

The hostage at the far end of the room was obviously a conscientious Muslim who belonged to the Sunni branch of Islam and performed prayers daily. When the guard approached him to cut his hair, he protested loudly and long. As a Muslim it would be shameful for his hair to be cut; he would no longer be able to perform his prayers with dignity. To have his head shaved as a prisoner was to indicate that he had done wrong, and sinners do not have the same standing at prayer. The guard had no sympathy for this argument and proceeded to shave the hair from his head in spite of his loud protest. I realized external appearance had much to do with a person's sense of inner value.

One day the guard said that a photographer had come to take my picture. I was placed against the wall, and a picture was taken with a Polaroid camera. The photographer was masked so that I could not see his face. Obviously my captors wanted to prove to the outside world that I was still alive. I took this incident as a possible sign of further progress toward my release.

On May 13, without announcement, I was told that I was going to be moved once again. I was allowed to go to the bathroom and then my hands were taped behind my back. My mask was removed and tissue paper was taped over my eyes—a secure blindfold. My arms were taped to my sides and my ankles were fastened loosely. During this time the guard said to his companion—though I thought he was really speaking to me—"He will be going home very soon to see his family." I grunted to show I had heard and assented. Then I was led out of the room, down a few steps, and up into a vehicle. The guard told me to sit. My feet were in a depression in the floor, probably the empty well for a spare tire. The guard proceeded to push me into this tire well. It was such a tight fit he had to cut loose a band of tape from my ankles, but after a lot of shoving he forced me into that narrow space.

It was decidedly uncomfortable. My position put particular pressure on my hands and shoulders, but I couldn't move. At least I was alive. The guard then put the floor covering over my face. I was encased in the tire well. The vehicle then started up and bounced over a rough road for twenty minutes or so. Finally we came to a stop inside a hollow-sounding building, a storage area or large garage.

I was taken out and the tape was taken off my hands. It was a relief to be able to move them again. But a series of wires was put around my neck, and objects were put into my pockets that I was told were explosives. The guard warned me that the driver would set off the explosives if I made any noise.

Then I was taped with heavy plastic tape from head to foot as on the first day of my kidnapping. My arms were taped to my sides, and the tape was wound around my head, allowing just enough space for me to breathe through my nose. I didn't like the experience any better the second time, but I said to myself, If I survived this once, I can do it again.

The guard said, "If you behave yourself and are quiet, you will be going home very soon. You may even be on your way today." I really doubted that it would happen the way he described, but I hoped he was right.

Then I was placed once again into the tire well and the cover was put back over my face. In spite of being taped like a mummy, I could move a little more than the first time. However, it was a very tight fit, and I was afraid to move very much because I didn't know the nature of the explosives in my pockets.

I was reminded of what the guard had said to me months earlier, after he had found me at the open window yelling for help: "I will put TNT in your pockets. I am going to tie you up and put you in the roadway. You will squirm and set off your own explosives and kill yourself." I hoped desperately that what was in my pockets was more stable than TNT.

I heard the driver get into the front seat and start the motor. A metal door lifted and the van moved out of the building. We were soon on a hard-surfaced highway, moving along at a good speed. Occasionally a rut or a large pothole in the road would jar me, and I found myself trying to protect both my face and my back.

A song came to mind from youth conferences many years before. "We are on the homeward trail, yes, we are on the homeward trail." The line ran joyfully through my head. But for me it had a double meaning. I could be moving back toward Beirut and release, going home to my family. Or some violent event might occur to cause my death. For me that meant being united with God in Jesus Christ, so I would indeed be home. I concentrated on the first possibility and felt a sense of joy that sometime in the near future I would join my loved ones.

We sped along, turning sharply into one road after another. At times we stopped for an extended period, perhaps at a roadblock. I rehearsed all the scripture verses and hymns that I could remember. This helped me focus on what lay ahead and not become frantic in my cramped and dangerous situation.

This time the ride over the mountains seemed much longer than before. We were probably taking the winding and circuitous route through the Damour River valley to the coastal city of Damour before going north. Eventually the winding curves ended and we seemed to be on the level, speeding over a highway I took to be the road leading north to Beirut. My hunch was confirmed by the increasing sounds of vehicles on the highway.

Aircraft motors and planes overhead told me we were close to the Beirut airport. The driver suddenly slowed down and turned onto a rough, unimproved road. The sound of a jet motor became louder and louder. The van stopped. I could hear a large metal door opening. We moved inside and the door closed. The driver wasted no time in getting out of his seat and moving back to where I was. He struggled for a minute or two to get the cover off the tire well.

When the cover lifted, I could feel the fresh air. He took me by the shoulders and tugged and tugged until I finally was free enough to be pulled out of the tire well and laid on the flat bed of the van. Then he cut off all the tape and allowed me to sit up, but I was still blindfolded. He went outside of the van, and soon came back, saying, "Here. Take this. It's a can of Pepsi." The cold, sweet liquid tasted oh, so good. I was then led out of the van and told to sit down on a mattress. The guard warned me to be very, very quiet, not even to whisper. I sensed that the guard was sitting behind me with a weapon in his hand. Several hours had gone by since I was taped and taken from the house in the Bekaa Valley, and the ride to the airport had taken a long time. Perhaps it was now late afternoon. As I sat on the mattress, I could hear someone using a grinding wheel. I was probably in a walled-off section of a repair shop in an airplane hangar.

The guard was very alert and did not even want me to move my position on the mattress. As time went by I realized that I had to urinate. I motioned to the guard. He was insistent that there was no way to relieve myself and I would just have to be patient. I sat there in considerable distress for what seemed to be two hours or more, trying to forget the mounting internal pressure. Occasionally another guard would come and whisper to my captor and then go away. Finally I heard the other guard say, "They will be here soon." I didn't know what that meant but tried to imagine that a plane was coming to take me to freedom. Finally the other guard said, "They're here. Let's go."

I was led from around the back of the van to the front and there told to get into a small vehicle. It was something like a small bathtub on wheels, just my length, with a hinged top. I assumed that it was either a small baggage carrier or the kind of vehicle used by vendors of soft drinks or sandwiches. I climbed into the space and lay on my back, and the top was closed over me. A motorcycle-type motor was started and the door to the hangar was opened. The vehicle moved rapidly over a hard surface and then we were on an unimproved road.

We continued to bounce, turn corners, and speed along for perhaps twenty minutes. Then we came to a halt and the lid was opened. I climbed out and was led across a pile of sand and down into the basement of a building. We walked upstairs to the second or third floor. I kept repeating in a whisper that I needed to go to the toilet.

Once in the apartment I was allowed to go to the toilet, but there was so much pressure on my bladder it took me two trips some twenty minutes apart. Then I felt much more comfortable. I had gone eight hours or more without the opportunity to relieve myself.

I was seated on a bed in a hallway and given a sandwich for the evening meal. Then I was taken to the corner of a passageway where there was a very thin mattress and told to lie down. My right ankle was chained and closed with a padlock. I was aware of a good deal of activity around me. There were many people in the apartment. From the rattling of pans and dishes in the kitchen I realized that there were at least two guards and maybe more. I was warned to keep very quiet. Finally the guards left the kitchen and went to the adjoining room to watch television. I tried to sleep, but I was not very comfortable because there was a board under the mattress that was narrower than the mattress itself. I finally found that I could sleep on my side.

I continued to live in that hallway for several days with people moving back and forth past me. They could not get through the narrow passage without stepping on my mattress. The second day a folded cot was placed next to me as a kind of barrier, making an improvised cubicle. At times I would slip my mask down to look around a bit. I could only see into the kitchen a few feet away. In front of me was a hallway leading to a very small bathroom. A few feet away to my right were the entrances to two rooms where the guards stayed and perhaps slept. In the morning a blanket was put over my head. I was told not to take it off. During that time I could sense that a guard was taking one hostage and then another to the bathroom and back again. I seemed to be able to count four different hostages.

Several different times a guard would notice that I was replacing my mask after having looked around and I would be scolded, but nothing more than that happened. One evening within a day or two of my arrival a man came into the apartment with a camera. I was told to stand against a wall and at a signal to remove my mask and look into the camera. When I did so, I found that the man's face was entirely hidden and I was looking into an instant camera with a flash. Then my mask was replaced.

Again I was encouraged to know that someone was interested in my picture. This gave me hope that some activity was going on for negotiating my release, but I told myself it would take time at the very best.

After some days I was moved from the hallway to the room on my right. There I found myself chained to a cot by both my left ankle and right wrist. The cot was enclosed in a cell formed by blankets hung over a wire at the foot of the bed and a shower curtain along the side. The bed was more comfortable and I was up off the floor. I also had privacy and didn't have to worry about people stepping on my mattress and me as they passed. In the same room there was a sofa on which a guard slept at night. One of the guards was talkative and would ask me about myself. He would even crack a joke or two. However, the guard who slept on the sofa was much more severe. The chain on my ankle was very tight and cut into the flesh, breaking the skin. At night I tried to stretch that leg out to place as little pressure as possible on it. When I did so, the bed creaked and the guard would wake up. He told me that I should make no noise. He suspected that I was trying to take the chain off and escape. That was obviously not possible, but he insisted that there would be no creaking of the bed. I looked forward to the nights when the other guard slept on the sofa.

In my cubicle I could take off my mask and look around. The floor was quite dirty and it had been dirty in the hallway too. I could hear the guards spitting on the floor. Eventually I could hear some of them beginning to cough and I could hear other coughing voices. My own throat became sore and I started to cough. I felt that I had a low fever. The virus was being passed around.

A doctor appeared one day and asked me how I felt. I said I had a cold but was otherwise in good health. He took my blood pressure and was pleasantly surprised to see that it was normal. He congratulated me on the good state of my health. The two guards also congratulated me on my physical well-being. (They should be congratulating my ancestors for the genes they gave me, I mused.) All during this time I did what I could to exercise and was glad to have the privacy of the cubicle. In spite of the chains I could do sit-ups, arm exercises, and some squatting motions to try to keep my circulation going.

The day after the doctor's visit the rhythm of the apartment changed dramatically. It was apparent that the guards were doing a massive cleaning of the floor. In typical Lebanese fashion they were pouring water and soap on the floor and then sweeping it down the drain. Then they mopped the floor with a disinfectant.

Every day after that saw mopping of the floor and use of a disinfectant. The doctor must have given them strict instructions. They also came to me with a spoonful of cough syrup, but by this time my cough had gone away. During these days and afterward I could hear the sound of airplane jet engines not far away. I assumed that I was being held in the southern suburbs, not far from the airport.

During Ramadan, a month in the Muslim calendar when there is fasting in the daytime and feasting at night, an effort was made to provide food (such as hamburgers) that non-Lebanese hostages would enjoy. I was given one hamburger in a paper bag with Arabic writing on it. It was from a store in Bourj al-Barajneh, near two large Palestinian camps. Some weeks later, when I had a chance to read an Arabic newspaper, I learned that two major militia groups had mounted an offensive against the Palestinians in these camps, to keep them from becoming a large armed force within the area.

The guards were very strict and even proud about their observance of the daytime fast during Ramadan. One of them explained that between sunrise and sundown they neither ate nor drank. It was considered reprehensible for a person even to swallow his own saliva —a rather extreme position. However, after sunset they entered into the customary feasting. This meant a large evening meal with special foods and a second large meal at the end of the night before dawn and the first prayer of the new day. Even so they provided me—and, I presumed, the other hostages—with food and drink at midday and late afternoon. Then after they had their evening feast, they would also bring some of their hearty meal, more than I really wanted to eat. There were special dishes in large quantities. They wanted me to know time and again that I was benefiting from the same good food they were eating. I was able to compliment them on these meals without hesitation. As I told them, I was accustomed to visiting my Muslim friends at this time of the year just as they visited me at Christmas and Easter.

18

"Do I have to wait 444 days for Ben's release?"

Ten months had gone by since Ben was taken. In order to make people aware of the plight of the hostages, I had to change from private person to public personality. This transformation was against my nature, but it was the only way to get action to help Ben and the others. John dropped his studies, and the church agreed to have him travel with me.

The report from Jeremy Levin and Ben's letter combined to convince us that Ben's life was really threatened. Arriving in New York, I called the State Department and asked to talk to someone concerned with the hostage question. I was told that I would have to talk with the Office of Counterterrorism. I didn't want to talk with anyone in counterterrorism. Such a view of Middle East problems focuses on the symptoms, not on the source of the trouble. Also, counterterrorism implies an exclusively military response. I told the staff person at the Lebanon desk that I wanted to talk with the person or persons responsible for the hostage issue. "If you want to talk about the hostages, you will have to talk to Mr. Robert Oakley, Director of the Office of Counterterrorism." I asked for an appointment with Mr. Oakley.

During this telephone call, I also asked for an appointment with Secretary of State George Shultz. I was told that I would be informed later if this was possible.

I contacted Catholic Relief Services, for whom Father Jenco served, and told them I would be going public. They said they understood but that they themselves would not take a public stance.

I thought back to the situation in Lebanon. In response to Israeli military attacks on Shiite communities, radicalized Shiites had formed resistance and suicide squads. The Israelis counteracted by an "iron fist" policy: homes were entered without warning, suspects were detained without trial, and people were executed without question.

A resolution now before the United Nations requested a fact-finding probe of the Israeli occupation force's actions against the civilian population and called for their withdrawal from south Lebanon. I telephoned the Lebanon desk of the State Department and asked about the resolution. How would the United States vote this time? A similar motion had been vetoed by our delegate when it had been introduced a few months earlier. I was worried about the climate of world opinion concerning the U.S. role in the Middle East. Ben had been kidnapped not because of anything he had done, not because he was a Christian missionary, but simply because he was an American. I believed that this kidnapping of Americans was a result of our lack of concern for justice in the area.

The Lebanon desk said that if the UN resolution condemned Israel, the United States would veto it. "No matter what Israel does, the United States will veto the resolution?" I asked. The answer came back: "If there is any language which condemns Israel, the United States will veto it."

I obtained a copy of the resolution from the United Nations and there was indeed language condemning Israel for sending forces to Lebanon and occupying south Lebanon. The United States vetoed the resolution.

The March 12 veto angered many Lebanese people. The United States had supported the Lebanese government, supplying arms, using the battleship *New Jersey* to shell Muslim positions, sending in the Marines, and training the Lebanese army. Now with this veto the Reagan Administration was opposing this same government. To the Shiites this was proof positive that the United States was Lebanon's enemy.

Our efforts to obtain the release of the hostages always faced a setback when relations between the United States and the Arab world worsened. The realization that by vetoing this resolution my government put Ben in more danger was depressing, to say the least.

John and I went to Washington, where I tried again to get an appointment with the Secretary of State. We were told that Mr. Shultz was in Moscow, attending the funeral of Konstantin Chernenko, but on March 15 we met with Richard W. Murphy, Assistant Secretary for Near Eastern and South Asian Affairs. The appointment was arranged by Bill Stanton, who was at the Lebanon desk of the State Department. He was gracious and very helpful. John, Fred, and I were ushered in to see Secretary Murphy. I had had Ben's letter duplicated and sent along to the State Department before our visit.

"Mr. Murphy," I asked, "what is happening on the hostage issue?"

"We don't know where they are or who has them," was the answer.

I have rarely seen Fred Wilson angry, but he was now. "Those are the very same words you used with me last September! How can it be that after all these months you have no other information."

Mr. Murphy had not seen Ben's letter. We gave him another copy and urged him to get in touch with the Kuwaiti government. Then we left, feeling depressed. There certainly was no sense of urgency here.

On March 16, Terry Anderson, Middle East correspondent for the Associated Press, was kidnapped in West Beirut, the third foreigner to be abducted in three days. Islamic Jihad claimed responsibility. These kidnappings occurred after the United States vetoed the resolution condemning Israel's policy in south Lebanon. (The other two who were taken were British citizens, and they were released later; Great Britain had abstained from voting on the UN resolution.)

The State Department response to Terry Anderson's kidnapping was to say that they had warned Americans to leave the country—and a number of embassy employees were in fact later evacuated.

My first U.S. appearance on Ben's behalf was in San Diego at a church council meeting, followed by a press conference. I said that Ben's abduction and his recent letters were cries of desperation from radicalized Lebanese who themselves had suffered severely. I pointed out that the Lebanese people had legitimate grievances against the United States for our involvement in their affairs, particularly our support of Israel. I further suggested that the terrorists represented people who were themselves suffering and who through violent acts were making a desperate attempt to be heard.

I reported that my meeting with Richard Murphy of the State Department had not yielded anything substantive. "The government has told me that they are working carefully and slowly. I have told them that I will accept 'carefully' but not 'slowly.' " My voice wavered a few times when I spoke about Ben, but I fought to keep my composure.

I completed my first press conference by asking, "Do I have to wait four hundred and forty-four days for Ben's release?" Four hundred and forty-four days was the length of time the hostages taken by Iranian militants from the U.S. Embassy in Tehran had been held. Could Ben possibly be held that long?

An appointment was finally arranged with Secretary of State George Shultz, so on March 21 I flew to Washington. John, Fred, Alvin, and I were escorted as a group by Bill Stanton. As we waited in a reception room, it was made clear to us that we would only have thirty minutes.

I can remember soft shades of green, dark polished wood floors covered with Persian rugs, sparkling chandeliers. There were beautiful paintings of scenes from American history. This room had been decorated by the Smithsonian Institution. It was a restful and elegant place in which to wait for our appointment.

We were ushered into a room where Secretary Shultz was sitting at a large table with several other people. I recognized Bernard Kalb. We had planned to divide our limited time. I would take the first fifteen minutes and the others the second.

Secretary Shultz began by saying that the hostage situation was very difficult and that maybe we had some suggestions. He expressed a sense of helplessness. No one knew exactly who the kidnappers were or how to contact them.

I had many questions on my mind and I was anxious to get his answers. I pressed him about doing something about the captors' demands for the release of the prisoners in Kuwait. The Secretary said that our administration would never interfere with another government. What Kuwait did was its own affair.

I suggested that the U.S. government negotiate with the people holding the hostages. Mr. Shultz said such people were crazy, they heard voices from God, they were deranged. It was impossible to talk to them.

I said I knew they were hostile, very angry and very determined, but they were not deranged. They were not out of touch with reality. It was possible to deal with them. Besides, it should be recognized that they had some legitimate grievances against the United States.

Mr. Shultz was angered by this whole exchange and pounded on the table. He indicated that the Shiites—who participate in a festival called the Ashura—demonstrate that they are pagan, primitive people.

John tried to offer a reasonable explanation of the Ashura, the Shiites' holiest days. He pointed out that it was an authentic expression of their faith and readiness for self-sacrifice in defense of their beliefs. Mr. Shultz said that in any case the government policy was not to negotiate with terrorists.

Alvin and Fred joined the discussion, pointing out that the pattern of calling for quiet diplomacy and repeated routine responses had been going on for many months, and we needed to see some progress. We wanted to be gentle, but we had to face the nonresponse of our government. The matter was urgent.

Our time was up too soon, and we were ushered out.

At a press conference following the meeting, I made Ben's letters to our church officials public for the first time and said the Administration was not doing enough. Serious negotiations were needed. The personal intervention of the President would be helpful. I would seek an appointment with the President.

Discouraged by our meetings in Washington, we went to the church, asking for special prayer services, one million postcards to the President, letters to senators and representatives, and media coverage. To enlist the help of people at a grass-roots level, I went on a tour of about twenty cities to talk to church groups and hold press conferences.

While the church groups were interested in the early days of our crusade, they often didn't know how to react. The initial response was low-key. We wanted the kind of concern that the Iranian crisis had stimulated in the public. Instead, listeners would sometimes focus their questions on details of Islamic theology or simple disbelief that our government wouldn't be doing all that it could.

Oscar McCloud accompanied John and me on a visit to Pittsburgh. After talking with two church groups, doing a radio interview on a car phone, and holding a press conference, we bumped into Dennis Benson (who helped us write this book) and Gregg Hartung, media professionals who produce radio and television programs for the church.

Dennis interviewed me for a syndicated radio program as we rode to the airport, and suggested that we record some voice segments for a series of radio spots, so John and I worked on these audio bits with him.

In the next four days, Dennis and Gregg produced a series of radio spots with music, sound effects, and narration. Oscar arranged for payment of distribution costs, and the spots were sent to every radio station in the country. The stations responded warmly to my personal appeal to listeners to help save Ben's life by writing to President Reagan. Over a thousand stations indicated that they were running these spots as public affairs announcements. Many stations called for phone interviews.

My confidence began to grow. With experience I became more comfortable in front of cameras and microphones. Reading the letter Ben sent about the danger to his life helped the audience connect to the situation emotionally. Every time I read it I was reminded of how much we had shared through the years, and I could feel tears welling up. After Jeremy Levin told us privately about the conditions of his own captivity, I could communicate the harsh reality of Ben's situation.

But I was getting more and more exhausted. John would try to get me to relax. "What other twenty-seven-year-old son follows his mother around the country?" he would say. I was grateful for John's help. He remembered details while I focused on the broad issues. He managed tickets and suitcases and went on numerous errands. He took his turn speaking in churches, meeting the press, and handling telephone calls. I couldn't have managed without him. I have a new appreciation for his good sense and good humor, his analytical mind and playful spirit.

One student at the seminary in Beirut had asked in an embarrassed but direct manner if Ben actually worked for the CIA. Nothing could be further from the truth. I guess that movies and spy novels have prepared people to see a government agent in everyone who works overseas. The questioner also assumed that Ben must have done something wrong in order to be taken. Now that I was in the United States I had to set the record straight here also: Ben had *not* worked for the government, and he certainly hadn't worked for the CIA. So in my presentation I included information about the important relief work for the Shiites Ben had undertaken at different points in our thirty-one years of serving the Lebanese people.

As interest grew in the hostage accounts, many people asked what they could do. We had already felt that some specific or directed action might help them respond. On March 19, 1985, the Presbyterian Church had endorsed a nationwide postcard-writing campaign. Church people were asked to send a postcard to the President with the plea that something be done for our hostages. Our goal was one million cards. Many congregations handed out postcards during the worship service. I recorded a tape with a one-minute appeal about sending cards that was often played during church services as cards were passed out. The sharing of my pain with this loving body of Christians was bearing fruit.

We never had any official word from the White House about how many postcards they received, although we asked several times, but one State Department official called Fred Wilson. "Please, stop the postcards." Fred asked him how many had come in. "We can't give you that information, but we have had to hire three new secretaries."

"When the hostages are released, the postcards will stop," Fred told him.

Our tour was going well. More and more newspaper articles started appearing as we became better known. The whole family did interviews. It was unnerving to sit before a reporter or talk to an interviewer by phone, wondering if they would get the story right. I was pleased by how professional and accurate the newspaper people were, but it was hard to get continued network coverage. I would have done just about anything to have a nightly reminder of the hostages such as that given by Walter Cronkite on CBS during the Iranian hostage crisis.

We were grateful to be able to meet several times with Robert Oakley, head of the Office of Counterterrorism in the State Department, and his staff. He was very personable. His children and ours had attended the same school in Lebanon, and he knew something about the people and the culture of the Middle East.

Mr. Oakley claimed that there were hundreds of people working on the hostage problem. That meant increasing intelligence, shoring up embassies, and trying to determine when an attack might take place. However, none of these things would help to obtain the freedom of the men being held. Why was the Reagan Administration so willing to sacrifice the lives of these men who had given of themselves in service? They were our country's best kind of "export." The government needed to have a single person in charge of this issue.

Mr. Oakley looked tired and overworked. He and his staff were boxed in by administration policies. It was impossible to try new approaches under the present outlook. Bargaining is a way of life in the Middle East. No one ever pays the first price asked. To deny these people the right to bargain was to challenge their humanity. One high government official admitted that he had not agreed with U.S. policy in the Middle East for the past twenty years. He himself had lived in the region and had personal knowledge of the people and their problems. How could he continue in his job if he had to compromise his values daily?

Toward the end of March, the family of Father Lawrence Martin Jenco, a large, warmhearted group, invited Terry Anderson's sisters and John and me to join them in Joliet, Illinois. We were starting to realize that we all had to work together to gain the release of the five being held. John and I were stepping up our media appearances, and the Jenco family was launching an awareness campaign: "Free the Hostages!" Peter Kilburn's family was in California and unable to be with us. Jeremy Levin and his wife, Sis, dedicated themselves to work with the other families after his "escape" in February. William Buckley, who had been held the longest, was a bachelor. We were never in touch with members of his family.

On March 30, Oscar McCloud, Fred Wilson, John, and I met at the New Canaan Baptist Church in Harlem. We had breakfast with the pastor, the Rev. Wyatt Tee Walker, the Rev. Jesse Jackson, and members of the congregation. After the service we agreed on an open letter to the Shiite community in Beirut. We would try to make contact with the kidnappers ourselves.

This meeting gave me a strong sense of support. The members of this congregation reflected the concern of the larger Christian community to which I belonged through Jesus Christ. They were lively, eager, and active in church service, welcoming me warmly as a stranger in their midst. Many promised to continue to remember us in prayer.

Rev. Jesse Jackson released a comprehensive statement about the Middle East that appealed for the release of the hostages in the context of a call for justice for the people of Lebanon. On April 17 the statement appeared in several Lebanese newspapers.

Americans didn't seem to understand why there is so much rage against us in the countries of the Middle East. I tried to explain that the captors who took Ben were angry at President Reagan. Our foreign policy worked against them, and they felt dominated and oppressed by our government's role in the area.

The fundamentalist Iranian Revolutionary Guards had not entered Lebanon until the Israeli invasion in 1982. The United States was implicated by its tacit approval of that military move. Our daughter Christine was a nurse at the American University Hospital during the time of the Israeli invasion, and she saw people coming into the emergency room with their bodies still on fire from American-made phosphorus bombs. The United States had supplied the Israelis with cluster bombs, vacuum bombs, and weapons of every kind. American bombs by air and American shells by sea were raining on the city of Beirut. The civilian population was on the verge of panic. We were under siege, trapped, intimidated, frightened, and threatened by this nightmare of massive artillery barrage. President Reagan finally called Prime Minister Begin in outrage over the intensity of this attack on the capital city, but only after eleven more hours of killing was there a cease-fire.

The same day the UN Security Council passed a resolution censoring Israel for the invasion of West Beirut. The United States abstained. The PLO at this point agreed to leave Beirut if the safety of Palestinian families left behind could be guaranteed. U.S. envoy Philip Habib assured the PLO that their families would be safe. However, the matter was left up to the Israelis. American marines escorted the PLO out of Beirut, which took ten days. The Israelis then allowed the right-wing Maronite Christian party, the Phalange, to enter the refugee camps. There followed the tragic massacres of the Palestinians at Sabra and Shatilla. Assurances of safety by the United States had not been honored, and many Arabs felt strongly that the United States was responsible.

Another reason for growing anti-American feeling was the increasing role our country took in Lebanon. We sent a "peacekeeping" force to the city, but our soldiers were authorized to fire on the Shiite and Druze people. Our fleet, including the battleship *New Jersey*, fired on Druze positions in the Shuf Mountains. Our planes provided air strikes at the request of the Lebanese government.

With all these grievances against Americans, a suicide truck driver rammed the U.S. Marine headquarters near the Beirut airport in October 1983 and killed 265 Americans. Islamic Jihad took the credit.

Muslim fundamentalists feel that the pressure of Western culture has tempted Muslims from the true way. Western music, seductive films, and other items of Western mass culture are seen as bad influences. The Iranian revolution inspired people through the simple means of cassette copies of speeches and sermons played from the local mosques. Perhaps the victory of fundamentalists in Iran could work elsewhere.

Whenever there was another act of aggression on the part of the Israelis, more young people in Lebanon were recruited into the movement for revolution. Our people in the United States could not grasp the flow of this pain and anger.

On a trip to Atlanta in April I was able to see former President Jimmy Carter. He said that as a former President he was not permitted to get involved in foreign policy, but he offered some sound advice. He was very gentle with the Reagan Administration. Perhaps he and his own staff had made many mistakes, he said. But it was clear to us that the families of the hostages seized in November 1979 at the U.S. Embassy in Tehran were treated very differently. During the Iranian crisis the families were gathered in Washington at the urging of the Carter Administration. They met with President Carter and with the First Lady, Rosalynn Carter, and were briefed on what was being done to obtain the freedom of their loved ones.

In order to stir action in our government, John and I visited Capitol Hill. At stake were the lives of five Americans (soon to be seven, with the seizure of David Jacobsen on May 28 and Thomas Sutherland on June 9). It was a bipartisan effort. The politics of the hostage family members differed. We hoped to gather support from both Republicans and Democrats.

Presbyterians and others were writing to their senators and representatives about the hostage crisis. This helped us get appointments. The lawmakers themselves might be elsewhere but most often we could see staff members, who were just as helpful. I was pleased and encouraged that in our democracy it is still possible to get action if there is an awareness that a constituency out there cares.

Representative Norman Y. Mineta listened to our story and appealed later to the Japanese government to intercede with Iran on our behalf. We visited the office of Senator John Glenn of Ohio, among others, a Presbyterian and an elder in his church. He had had some experience in obtaining the release of an American held in Asia, and his staff gave John and me some excellent advice. We learned that it is hard for senators and representatives to gain access to the Administration. One way is to write a "Dear Colleague" letter and have it signed by as many senators and representatives as possible.

Senator Glenn wrote his own letter to the Secretary of State, inquiring about efforts to release Ben and the others. Weeks passed, but he did not get an answer.

The senators who spent the most time with us were Senators Jesse Helms of North Carolina and Paul Simon of Illinois. Senator Helms called all the hostage families together, telling us that we were one family in this crisis. He said that he had a box of matches in his pocket and that he would light them under Mr. Reagan if there was no action soon. He assigned a staff person to be in touch with us and gave us a list of nongovernmental agencies with Middle East connections. He and his staff encouraged us to make a videotape with appeals by all family members. The tape was sent to Lebanon and shown on television there.

We wanted to have a media event and pointed out to our friends on the Hill that on May 8 Ben would have been held one whole year. So on that day Senator Helms gathered the hostage families together, escorted us to the Senate chamber, and introduced us to Senator Dole, the majority leader. (John later chastised me for not delivering a speech to him at that moment.) We were getting signatures for our "Dear Colleague" letter, but Senator Dole did not sign.

The chaplain of the Senate offered a prayer for the hostages. Robert Dole introduced the issue, and Jesse Helms and others spoke. The Senate chamber seemed dark and musty. Only a few senators were there.

Senator Paul Simon and his staff met with us several times. He arranged a meeting with Rev. Jesse Jackson and the hostage families. On April 18 he spoke in the Senate on the American captives in Lebanon, addressing his remarks to President Reagan. "The families of these distinguished men pray and anxiously plead for their safe release."

John and I were at a hotel in Chicago when we received a phone call from the State Department. An article in an Arabic newspaper in Kuwait claimed that a journalist had visited a basement in a partially constructed building in West Beirut where three of the kidnapped Americans were being kept. The writer of the article brought out a handwritten letter to me signed by Ben.

Dear Carol and family,

I thank God I am still alive and in the Spirit have celebrated Easter with you. I think of you often and thank God for your love and faith as I am sure that you and your friends pray for me. I am sure God is with you and me, and that his will is good, acceptable, and perfect.

I love you very much and thank God that he sustains us with his everlasting grace and love.

Affectionately,

Benjamin M. Weir

It was written on a sheet of notebook paper that folded out so that on one side was my letter and on the other side the following letter:

Dear Carol,

I am well and your two messages have been received. I am here because of American political policy in support of Israel, and because of opposition to it others are prisoners in Kwait [sic]. Thus far the US government has not responded positively, but is able to do so. I ask you to do what you can to persuade the US government to put pressure on Kwait [sic] to release those prisoners. I understand that if the US government does not put pressure on Kwait [sic] to release those prisoners, then my life will be in danger and I will hold the U.S. government and President Regan [sic] responsible. I ask you to act quickly because it is very hard for me to continue in this situation.

Sincerely,

Benjamin M. Weir

Was this letter dictated to Ben by someone? Did the misspellings indicate that he was rushed or tired? Were there clues in it? It was so exciting to receive a personal note from him. It seemed too good to be true. It was upbeat and sounded just like him.

The newspaper article further claimed that the reporter had reliable information about a mediation process carried out by a third nation.

When the State Department was approached by the media, they gave their stock answer about doing everything possible. Christine called the paper in Kuwait from Saudi Arabia and asked to talk with the reporter who had visited Ben. The staff insisted no one there knew the reporter. He worked in Jerusalem.

I had been requesting an appointment with President Reagan for some time. He was really the only person who could change the government's no-negotiations policy. His media power could encourage a public response to the plight of the hostages. I received the following letter, written April 30:

> *Dear Mrs. Weir,*
>
> *Thank you for your recent letter to the President asking to meet with him about your husband.*
>
> *I regret to write that, unfortunately, due to heavy commitments, we are unable to arrange a personal meeting for you with the President.*
>
> *We are glad that you have met recently with a number of top Administration officials, including Secretary of State Shultz, who reassured you we would pursue every available avenue to effect the safe release of your husband and the other American kidnap victims.*
>
> *With kind regards,*
> *sincerely,*
>
> *Frederick J. Ryan, Jr.*
> *Director, Presidential*
> *Appointments and Scheduling*

I was very disappointed not to meet with President Reagan, and I continued to try to see him. This I was never able to do. I knew it would be difficult for the President to see me. He was elected just at the end of the Iranian hostage situation, and at the time he said that he would never have such a crisis. He had asked then for an investigation into what had happened to keep Americans hostage for 444 days. It would be 495 days before Ben's release.

Two days before the first anniversary of Ben's captivity. I was in St. Louis. In a press interview I made the point that the lack of public awareness of the kidnapping was in sharp contrast to the constant attention given the Iranian hostages during their 444 days of captivity. Then, yellow ribbons had become a symbol across the country. Now I wore one on all my journeys.

19

"There is an inaccuracy. . . .
My wife and son could not possibly have been
to that many places."

One day there was a good deal of excitement among the guards.
I supposed that they were expecting some official in their group. Not
until months later did I learn that they were talking about TWA
Flight 847, which was hijacked June 14, 1985, on a flight from Athens
to Rome.

During these weeks I could hear explosions in the distance, and
there were the sounds of artillery rounds and large weapons being
fired in the vicinity at night. As time went on, the sounds came so
much closer it became evident that we were on the edge of a battle
zone. One day two large barrels of sand were placed in the bathroom.
This left very little space to move around. At the same time, in the
room where I was kept, twenty barrels were stacked up in a row
along the wall around the guard's bed and filled with sand. I assumed
that they were to provide some protection for him in case artillery
shells should explode nearby. It was not a very comforting thought.

More than once during that night I heard near at hand a truck-
mounted rocket launcher fire a salvo. I counted thirty reports. Like
the other vehicles it would move away. However, I knew that inevitably there would be incoming artillery.

After the second or third day, the guard brought me a flak vest. He
said, "Put it on and leave it on!" Wearing it was uncomfortable in the
hot and humid weather. When explosions shook the building, I would
be taken into an inner room. I could sense that there were others
there at the same time. One guard explained to me that they had
gone out and bought these vests at a cost of more than $100 apiece
for the hostages, but they themselves did not have them. This was
more evidence that they wanted me and the other hostages to live.

When I was moved to this apartment in Beirut, a very important
event occurred. Some days after I had been there I asked for a Bible.
I had been without any scripture for three months. To my surprise,
a guard brought me a book two or three days later. When I opened

it, I found the Revised Standard Version of the Old and New Testaments in English! This was a cause for great joy. I devoured that book every minute I had it. After I read it for some hours, the guard would take it, and it would not be available for another day or two. I surmised that it was being circulated among other hostages.

I read the Bible through from cover to cover more than once, but I found the psalms especially meaningful. When the psalmist spoke of being in a mirey pit and feeling that he was sinking, I knew that experience. When he spoke of a dark night and a lack of light, I could relate that to being kept under a blanket for an hour or more.

Again and again, the psalmists yearned for deliverance and freedom. This was my prayer also. But in the midst of their trying circumstances they found hope and a sense of God's salvation. Such a feeling became meaningful for me as well.

After reading the whole Bible, I turned to the introduction to the Revised Standard Version—the glorious history of those who through the generations have worked at preserving and understanding the biblical text, especially William Tyndale, who was burned at the stake for translating the New Testament into vernacular English. I could no longer think of the English text as just another book.

During this time one of the guards took particular interest in the fact that I spent so much time reading the Bible. This was the guard who warned me not to move on the springs of the bed or make any sound when he slept on the sofa.

One day he came and stood by my bed, pressing his finger hard against my forehead. I think he intended to irritate me, and he succeeded. I asked him to remove his hand, but he continued to press. He said I was bad and deceptive and deserved to be killed. He put his pistol against my cheek so I could feel the end of the barrel. He claimed I taught hatred of Muslims and encouraged armed militia groups to attack Muslim people. I assured him this was not true. I had many Muslim friends and would not want to do them harm. In fact, I had worked with a number of different Muslim groups during times of crisis to provide emergency aid to their people.

He would not hear this and said it was a fabrication. Finally, in a long diatribe he said that Christianity was false, it was not according to the truth; the Bible and the Gospel were fiction, and I was destined to burn in the fires of hell.

A few days later the director of the guards came and sat on my bed. (He was called Hajj by the guards as a sign of respect. He had not made the pilgrimage [*hajj*] to Mecca but was respected for his piety and authority.) He asked me how I was doing. I told him that the food was good, that I was in good health, and I only wished that I could be released to go home. He asked me how the guards were treating

me. I said, "On the whole, well," because this was true. I did not raise
the exception of the one who had been belligerent. After a short time
the Hajj got up and left.

Soon the guard who had been a problem came and asked in considerable detail what the Hajj had asked. I told him. He was concerned
about whether I had talked to the Hajj about him. I said no. From
that time on this guard no longer engaged in belligerent behavior.
Perhaps the Hajj had gotten wind of his disrespectful attitude from
one of the other hostages.

From time to time this guard would still come by and show me his
new pistol and explain how much it cost and how much power it had.
He wanted me to admire his toy. He was proud of it and yearned for
affection and attention. I found it impossible to admire the weapon,
but I told him I held no grudge against him. I said I hoped he would
find fulfillment in life and a more fruitful occupation.

One day in July a guard came in and asked if I wanted to see a
television program. I was delighted. He unlocked my chains, saying,
"I will take you to see the TV program."

I got up with my blindfold on, and he led me by the hand through
a series of passageways. He told me to sit on the mattress on the floor
and then offered me the greatest surprise. "You have a friend next
to you. Take his hand." I reached out into the space next to me.
Another hand met mine. I was holding the hand of another human
being!

The guard then told me to take off my blindfold. I did. I looked into
the face of the man next to me. He had a full beard just like me, The
guard was behind us, out of our sight. He asked who the man was.
I said I didn't know. I did not remember having seen him before.

We were ordered to watch the TV in front of us. It was a videocas-
sette on how a Muslim prepares for prayer. I couldn't concentrate
because I wondered who the person next to me was. The tape went
on for twenty minutes or so.

The guard told us to put our blindfolds back on, and he led me out.
I wondered what this was all about. I was curious. I didn't know who
this person was. I went to sleep pondering this strange experience.
I was awakened in the middle of night and told, "You are going to
be moved."

The guard led me outside and along a walkway, upstairs, and into
a room. I was seated on a mattress and chained to a wall. He said that
I was going to find a friend. The guard went out and locked the door.
I lifted my mask. To my surprise, I was in the room with the man I
had seen earlier. He was chained to the opposite wall.

I asked him in a whisper who he was and he said, Father Martin
Jenco. I introduced myself. He was as surprised as I was. We were

both stunned. The experience of being in communication with another person was so different from the loneliness of the past months that I was very suspicious. Was this some kind of trick in a bugged room? Were they trying to get information about us? Yet I was so pleased to be with someone else. Here was human companionship after so long.

We started talking in whispers. We shared things about our lives. He had read of me before his capture, which took place on January 8, 1985, eight months after mine. We joked and cried. We shared the same faith. We had had common experiences. There were concerns and fears to share. It went on and on. Our communication just kept picking up in tempo. There seemed to be no end to what we had to say. Great emotions seemed to overflow. I was communicating with another human being after fourteen months.

I learned that Father Martin had also been kept in isolation. For a long time he had not had any companionship either. We were quietly establishing a close and intimate relationship. I asked him, "Why do you suppose that this is happening?" The guards had never permitted this kind of interaction in the past. I still wondered if the room had a listening device. Will they soon separate us and pump each of us for information about the other? "I think that this place is bugged! Look at that thing down by the wall."

Father Martin didn't say anything for a while. He reached out to the spot where I had pointed. He picked it up and examined the object for a few seconds. Then he observed, with a shrug and a smile, "It's just a solid air freshener to make the room smell better." We laughed and laughed over my paranoia. My sides were hurting. I had not really laughed in fourteen months! I had cried, and I had occasionally smiled to myself, but I hadn't laughed. Now we joined in laughter, one of God's most incredible gifts.

Father Martin and I were pleased that we were not only in a room together, but a room that had intake and exhaust fans. Although the room was hot, it was bearable. Because of the noise of the fans it was difficult to hear each other. However, this kept our conversation from the guards outside.

It was amazing how naturally we moved to prayer after our laughter. God's joy had revealed itself, and our natural response was worship. After two hours we were emotionally exhausted by this burst of community and sharing. Finally we dropped off to sleep.

The next morning we awoke and exercised for a half hour before breakfast. We talked about the events of the night before and the noises we were hearing in the hallway. We wondered if there were more hostages nearby. We also made plans to worship after breakfast. I asked Father Martin to direct us in the celebration of Mass. He agreed and saved a piece of bread from breakfast, but insisted that I lead worship the following day.

By the next day we were convinced that there were other people next door to us. The guards were busy knocking on the walls, which we assumed was to fix metal rings to which chains could be attached. We were also allowed to read the Bible in English for a time; then it would be taken away, as if others were to have it. Later Father Martin was taken out by a guard. When he returned, he said he had been taken next door to hear confession from a Catholic layman: Terry Anderson, Middle East correspondent for the Associated Press.

Father Martin learned that David Jacobsen, administrator of the American University Hospital in Beirut, was also a hostage in the same room. He said that Terry Anderson had been reading the Bible to David, who did not have his eyeglasses. Father Martin also revealed that the two men were asking for permission for all of us to worship together. After he returned, he began asking for the same opportunity.

One July morning, a day or so later, the Hajj came again and sat on my mattress. He told me that he had an article from the daily Arabic newspaper to read to me.

The long article described an event that had taken place the previous March. The writer recounted the visit my wife, Carol, and son, John, had made to Washington, D.C., along with a representative from the Presbyterian Church, to meet with Secretary of State George Shultz to make a plea for greater efforts on behalf of myself and the other hostages. The article reported that in the course of the conversation they had called into question the U.S. policy toward the Middle East, and particularly the Arab countries. The Hajj read my son's report that at the end of the meeting the Secretary of State became furious with the suggestion that the Administration wasn't doing enough for the hostages and the pursuit of peace. Carol and John were reported to have pressed the unresolved issue of the future of the Palestinians as a root cause for terrorism in the Middle East. This had been particularly unacceptable.

The article went on to report how John and Carol had visited various American cities and publicized the plight of the hostages, which was relatively unknown to the general public. It listed twenty cities where they had traveled on this quest. I found this most surprising and said to the Hajj, "You have to realize that there is an inaccuracy in the article. My wife and son could not possibly have been to that many places." Little did I realize at the time that they had in fact traveled very widely and a considerable body of concern had developed. The 11,000 congregations of the Presbyterian Church (U.S.A.) were particularly aroused.

One day one of the guards came in the curtained-off part of the large room in which I was staying and asked, "What is the main theme of Christianity?"

I paused for a moment. "The main theme of Christianity is love. We are told in many different ways about the love of God. This love is for everyone, not just for Christians. We know that God has loved us very deeply by sending Issa [Jesus] to teach us about God's love.

"Jesus told us that God loves everyone. So when he healed the sick, preached to the poor, and associated with the outcasts of society, he was demonstrating that God loves everyone. Furthermore he taught us to love one another. In the story of the good Samaritan, he showed us that we are to be kind and loving to everyone who is in need. We are to regard everyone as our neighbor and to realize that his or her interests are as important as our own. Moreover, we know that God will save us from sin and give us new life if we commit our lives to him and believe the message of Jesus. This is why the New Testament teaches us that God is love."

The guard responded that he could not believe that God is simply love. Love is a very changeable emotion. One day you like someone, but the next day you are angry with him. In a family you can get along easily with some members but not with others. Love is very changeable but God is not changeable. Love is weak but God is strong.

He went on to say, "We know what is right as Muslims. That is why we are *ahil al mustakim* [people of the straight way]. We read the Koran and know what to do. We are told to believe in the one God so we believe in him. We know that all of life is to be surrendered to God.

"We follow the will of God in every detail. We know how to wash correctly before prayer and how to perform our prayers. We know what to eat and what not to eat. We know how long our beards are to be and we trim them accordingly. In every way we live the life of faithfulness to the will of God. You Christians are very lax. You drink alcohol, which is against the teachings of the Koran. In the Western countries you do not raise your children with strictness. Men and women go to the beach together. You allow your women to wear clothes which reveal their bodies. In many ways you do not live according to the will of God. But we know what is right and we are the people of the right way."

Once again I was dismayed at the radical difference in perspective about faith in daily life. I respected the Muslims' sense of dedication and desire to be found in the will of God. But I wished for them a greater sense of freedom and openness to consider other alternatives. I was also disappointed that there were no extended opportunities for exploring together the meaning of faith and trust in God in daily life.

That night after we were asleep, the guard's unlocking of the door awakened us, and I sat up blindfolded. I could hear the guard lay down a mattress and direct a person to sit. He then chained him to the wall and went out. After the door was locked I raised my mask and found that Father Martin was also looking at the new arrival. He was Thomas Sutherland, Dean of the School of Agriculture at the American University of Beirut. He said that he had been held for about five weeks in an underground area and only that night moved out to join us. He was as glad to see us as we were to greet him.

Tom said that he had not been able to sleep comfortably for many nights because the bed he was in was not long enough to accommodate his full length. Finding the isolation of that underground cell extremely difficult, he was now overjoyed to be with two other men. Tom was full of question and comments. We spent a couple of hours conversing until finally we went back to sleep.

After a few hours a guard awakened us for morning exercise. Then we had a meal together. Tom had been raised in Scotland and like myself was a Presbyterian, a member of the Presbyterian Church in Fort Collins, Colorado. I understood he had been Dean of the College of Agriculture at Colorado State University before coming to Beirut.

Tom was a very able teacher, and we began to learn many things from him. He opened new doors of understanding in his special fields of animal husbandry and genetics, and we learned a great deal about his experiences in Ethiopia and Nigeria. He also brought news of Carol that overwhelmed me. He reported that he had met her neighbors the previous fall, who said that she had left for the United States. Now I knew she was alive and well.

Father Martin, Tom Sutherland, and I became intimately acquainted as we slept and ate together in the same room. We also continued to ask daily if we could worship with the other men. One day we talked earnestly about this opportunity of worship. Again, we asked the guard if this could be possible.

By the end of the first week, the guard told us that there would be a gathering of all the prisoners and that Father Martin would lead the worship. When the time came, the guards led us, one by one, to another room. They would not let us remove our blindfolds. We could shake hands but not say anything. The guards told us to sit down with our backs against the wall.

Again they provided an English translation of the Bible.

Father Martin was permitted to remove his blindfold and read from the Bible; then he led us in the Mass. He passed out bread, but there was no wine. Thus we celebrated Mass together in the presence of two armed guards. We could hear them occasionally cock their weapons. We were permitted to hug each other before the guards led us out. It had been a very powerful experience, and I wept through part of it.

The following day I asked if we could worship together again. The guard said that we could do it sometime. Finally it happened about a week later. I was told that I would lead worship. I led the service according to my memory of the Presbyterian Book of Common Worship. I missed my worship book. I had not memorized the Communion service as Father Martin had the Mass.

I read from Paul's account in 1 Corinthians 11 of the Last Supper and served Communion. We sang very softly because the guard didn't want us to make much noise. I also read Psalm 103, "Bless the LORD, O my soul; and all that is within me, bless his holy name!" The guards kept rushing us along. When we finished, we hugged each other as a sign of God's peace.

Each day Father Martin and I asked for an opportunity to worship. About ten days later the guards collected all of us in the same room again. Then they told us to worship; we could remove our blindfolds once they closed the door. We were on our own! We were five in a locked room about ten feet square. When our mattresses were on the floor, we had very little space to walk around. During the day we would put our mattresses against the wall or stack them in the corner so that we would have freedom to exercise.

We now had an opportunity to share experiences. Father Martin led the worship service one day, I the next. We all took turns reading scripture passages. Each evening we prayed together again. We spoke of family members about whom we had special concern. Colleagues, other people in Lebanon, and ourselves were included. It was a deeply moving experience. We began to feel like real brothers, worshipers in "the church of the locked door."

David Jacobsen and Terry Anderson brought to our room their tradition of taking "walks." We continued this practice by taking a rapid walk around the room for thirty or forty minutes in the morning. We would do it again in the afternoon or perhaps again in the evening for a change of activity and some exercise. And there were always times for conversation.

In early August, unexpectedly, we were moved to a room downstairs in the basement. The upstairs room had had small intake and exhaust fans. The circulation made the hot summer more bearable; we had noticed the difference at those times when the electricity was cut off and we had no light or ventilation. However, we now were in a basement room with no circulation of air. Fortunately our captors allowed us to have a fan in the room. At those times when the electricity failed we not only lacked ventilation and light but were soon sitting in pools of sweat. On more than one occasion our mattresses were soaked with perspiration and we could find no way to dry them out. In the dark with the electricity off we were sometimes allowed to have a candle, but that only added to the hot temperature of the room.

The basement room was about the same size as our previous room. Although we were very crowded, we were glad to have the companionship. The door to the room did not go all the way to the floor. Usually one of the guards would bring food at dinnertime and slide it under the door. To receive the food, one of us would get on his hands and knees and take the bread or whatever was offered. The posture almost seemed like begging for food.

Unlike the upstairs room, the basement space had two small Arab-style toilets flush with the floor, a washbasin, and a shower. Even so, we were rushed to use the bathroom. The guard would only give us ten minutes each to wash clothes, take a shower, and clean our dishes. There never seemed to be enough time for the basic needs. We often wondered why the guards were so insistent on our getting so little time to use the bathroom once a day. As far as we could tell, the guards simply did not want to spend much time waiting for the prisoners. Though occasionally when the Hajj came to talk with us he would promise that we would have more time, it never seemed to happen.

From the beginning, the guards always carried weapons. Usually they seemed to be carrying submachine guns, but sometimes one of them would have a pistol. Occasionally one of the guards would come into the room, cock his weapon, and pull the trigger on an empty chamber. This was always an unnerving experience because we were never sure there would not be a round in the chamber.

Often for our morning breakfast we would each have a piece of cheese wrapped in tinfoil. Terry Anderson began to save the foil and then cleverly fashioned a set of chess pieces from it. When his chess set was completed, he asked for a piece of cardboard so that he could rule it off and play chess with a partner. At first the guards seemed to think that they would be able to do this. However, the cardboard did not appear. Terry kept asking for it. Then one of the guards said he would have to ask the person in charge whether we would be permitted to play chess or not. He explained that according to their Shiite Islamic rules they were allowed to do some things as guards but not others. He went on to say that we were expected to be governed by those same rules. The way in which the guards trimmed and cared for their beards would also be the way we were groomed. He would have to ask whether the guards could play chess as a way of finding out if the prisoners could play. We waited a number of days until finally the answer came. It was negative. A *fatwa*—a religious ruling —had been given. The guards and ourselves could play checkers but not chess. Their form of checkers, called *dama,* did not require much time to complete, but chess could be expected to occupy perhaps hours and that would be a waste of time. Terry was disappointed that he could not make use of his cleverly designed chess pieces. The rest of us were also unhappy with this decision. *We* had plenty of time.

On another occasion Terry saved from breakfast small cartons that the cheese came in. When he had a number of them, he proceeded, over a number of hours, to create a deck of cards with a ballpoint pen that had been given to us. When the deck was completed, we played rounds of hearts. A guard came suddenly into the room. He was first surprised and then angry to see us playing cards. He said that this was a forbidden activity and took the cards and destroyed them. Once again we were disappointed.

Sometime in mid-August we were given a notebook and a ball-point pen. It was one way in which an English word that was in question could be clarified with the guards. It also offered the opportunity to write in Arabic a phrase they wanted us to know. In the previous weeks we had surprisingly been given an outdated English-language newspaper. Each time there was a newspaper we read it through avidly word for word to glean from it whatever information we could find. It was our only contact with the outside world. Toward the middle of August the guards would occasionally allow me to have an Arabic newspaper. I would read through the headlines and tell the others what the topics were. When there was a topic of interest to all of us, I would read the entire article aloud, in translation. This aroused Terry's interest in learning Arabic. He began working at it very methodically, and I did what I could to help him. He prepared flash cards from cheese cartons. On them I would write words and phrases in Arabic with the translation. We began studying a few newspaper articles together. He worked at it very assiduously. I would read a line from the newspaper and he would repeat it after me. We could only do this for a limited time because it proved aggravating to the others, who were not interested in studying Arabic themselves. One exception was Tom Sutherland, who spent some days learning from Terry what he had learned from me. The guards were pleased at this interest, and when I made a mistake or did not complete a phrase for Terry to their satisfaction, they would take over and become his teacher.

Tom Sutherland had a very good command of French, so that

when an occasional French-language newspaper came into our hands, he shared that information with the rest of us. In these and other ways we found that we had interests and talents which complemented one another and helped to round out our gathered life.

Each day we spent considerable time exercising together. We even took imaginary trips. Sometimes David Jacobsen would take us to his apartment and cook a meal for us. We spent a whole evening there through our imagination. Another time Father Martin took us on a trip through Rome and we saw the well-known sites, restaurants, and churches. We ended up at his Servite order's house in Rome on a feast day! We had a wonderful meal and really celebrated. It was a very good time.

Tom Sutherland took us back to his native Scotland. First he would recite some Bobbie Burns poetry and then take us touring through a part of the country. The trek concluded with a fine imaginary meal. Terry Anderson took us to Japan with all its sights, tastes, and smells. There was great richness and depth to our sharing. In it were both playfulness and creativity. In the process we learned more about one another.

Either Father Martin or I would save a piece of bread from our morning meal for the Communion service. He would refer to this bread as "Jesus being nearby." He had a delightful sense of humor. His favorite saint was Saint Anne. When he couldn't find his medicine or he misplaced something, he would say that Saint Anne was playing games with him. This kind of thinking was a real part of his life.

I believe that the guards brought us together because they saw it had a positive impact on us. Their job was to keep us alive and healthy. The worship obviously contributed to this goal. It was also easier to manage five happy people than to control five angry or depressed prisoners. But I didn't know what their ultimate purpose was regarding us.

I later learned that we were brought together at the time that the Reagan Administration was negotiating for release of the hostages from hijacked TWA Flight 847. Did our captors think that the President would hold out for the release of all of those who were held hostage in Lebanon? If so, they would have been preparing us for release. We would be in better shape after being together than when we were kept in isolation.

In late August a few English books were brought for us to read. In one way or another they all centered on topics the guards thought we ought to know. Some of the books were about the Iranian revolution, others about the history and the development of Shiite religious thought. One book, by a Columbia University professor, dealt with the misunderstanding of Islam in the West. All these books were scholarly works written by university professors except for one, a doctoral thesis on the history of the Druze religion. We all read these books. Some I pondered for days at a time.

I spent a considerable amount of time on the book dealing with the development of Shiite religious thought. It was an intricate and difficult book, but I felt I wanted to know more about their historical background.

Occasionally one of the guards, whose name was Said (pronounced Sah-eed) would explain some aspect of Shiite Islam to us. He had completed the baccalaureate level of high school and had a quick mind. Much of his conversation had to do with the history of the twelve Imams or martyrs of the Shiite branch of Islam or some aspect of their religious rules and the reasons for their observance. He had also attended a few lectures in logic, and he was convinced that logical proposition was the way to win every argument.

He was quite proud of the fact that he was able to overcome every objection or question that might be raised about the topics he discussed in our informal seminar. The underlying assumption was that Islam is much better than Christianity, but there was never any serious intent to get any of us to become Muslims. Usually there was an atmosphere of give-and-take as one or another of us would explain something about our view of Christianity or our traditions. In many of these discussions I found myself in an intermediatory role. I was the only one in the group who knew Arabic, and the guard had a limited knowledge of English. He was forever asking me to provide English equivalents for Arabic words. He delighted in discovering my mistakes or inadequacies, and he never let me forget them. My response would often be that since he knew English and Arabic so well, he really didn't need my help. He would agree jokingly and then once more ask me when he got stuck for a word or phrase.

What bothered us most was the unpredictability of the guards and the fact that they would without hesitation lie to us. For instance, we were given a large plastic container of drinking water and told that it was to last us two days. From it we would each fill our own small plastic drinking containers. Many times the water would be finished, but still the guard would be unwilling to get us more until the better part of a day had passed. This behavior always made us angry and disappointed and taught us not to believe him when the guard said he would bring water in five minutes. Frequently we would ask one guard for fruit or tomatoes and be told there was none. Yet when we asked another guard, he would bring us what he had.

I was never able to determine exactly how many guards I came in contact with during my imprisonment, but I assume there were fifteen or twenty.

We continued to live in the basement room in the month of August. Often the building shook; we were not far from an area of serious fighting. This may be why we were kept there.

About the first of September we were moved back upstairs to the small room we had occupied in July. This was a more comfortable room with better ventilation, and we were glad to be "back home." Shortly before the move upstairs there were several gifts. Both David Jacobsen and Father Martin were provided with reading glasses. Fortunately I still had my own pair of eyeglasses.

Throughout the months of July, August, and September it had become clear that our guards were not happy with their task of watching us. From time to time they would say, "You want to go home, but so do we. We are confined here taking care of you. When the day comes that you are free, we will be free also."

I came to realize that they were captives of the system of which they were part as much as we were. They had probably been attracted to this group simply because they were unemployed and had no prospect of other work. The militia, like all other militia groups, would pay them a monthly wage. It might not be adequate, but at least it would sustain them. I learned by overhearing their conversations that initially each of them was paid about twelve hundred pounds a month—about $27 in U.S. money. As inflation soared, some got as much as fifteen hundred Lebanese pounds a month, or about $34.

Occasionally there was an activity none of us liked. The guard with the least education, who was the most unstable, would assemble us in the hallway outside our room and make us sit on the floor. He taught us a phrase in Arabic that is a kind of theme in Islam: *Allahu akbar* (God is great). He would have us stand up with each man's hands on the shoulders of the man in front of him. He would then march us up and down the hall in step, requiring us to say in Arabic, "One, two, *Ya* Hussein" (one of the martyrs of Islam); "three, four, *Allahu akbar.*" He would keep us at this for five or ten minutes or until he was tired. Then he would march us back in the cell. We considered this stupid and a form of mocking us.

On other occasions this guard, in the early morning as we awoke, would bring to us small Arabic coffee cups and delicious black Arabic coffee. It was a welcome and wonderful treat, but we soon learned that the guard thrived on appreciation and would become belligerent if he felt that he did not receive enough thanks.

I learned to express my delight and surprise as soon as he brought the coffee and to thank him again and again throughout the day. This seemed to appease the incipient anger which was always just below the surface in his relationship with us. He was the same guard who earlier had belittled my view of Christianity. He never harmed me physically, and I came to learn that he not only had difficulties relating to our small group but also to the other guards.

20

"Go right on doing what you are doing."

John and I were able to get an appointment with Robert C. McFarlane, National Security Adviser, on May 8, exactly one year after Ben was kidnapped. Fred Wilson was not included, but we took him with us. After going through security, we were escorted to the Old Executive Office Building and introduced to Lt. Col. Oliver North. Representatives of the Jenco family joined us as Colonel North walked with us to an adjoining room to meet Mr. McFarlane.

We were offered coffee. This welcome show of hospitality reminded me of the thick black Arabic coffee always offered over business transactions in the Middle East. Nervous and edgy, I was always hopeful that each new encounter would be good news for us.

His speech slow and deliberate, his manner and words controlled, Mr. McFarlane sought to reassure us. The Administration was working in three directions: improving its intelligence work, pressing allies to help, and leaving open the possibility of contact with Iran. I had read in newspaper accounts that the United States had threatened Iran with military retaliation if American citizens held hostage were put on trial or executed. I expressed my distaste at this possibility since I didn't believe the kidnappers were under the direct control of Iran. Instead, particularly for the sake of what help Iran might offer, I believed we needed normal diplomatic relations with that country.

We were assured by Mr. McFarlane that everything possible was being done for the release of the hostages, and not long after that when I told Mr. McFarlane I didn't want to deal with the State Department any longer, Colonel North was assigned to be our contact. This legendary soldier had many clandestine activities associated with his name.

Fred continued to be in touch with Terry Waite. Twice before we had offered our own negotiator to the Administration, once in July 1984 and again in November. Twice we had been turned down.

Terry promised he would stop in New York on his return to London from a trip to Australia with the Right Reverend Robert Runcie, the Archbishop of Canterbury. True to his promise, he met with us on May 10, in the office of the Episcopal Church, along with several Episcopal Church officials. Fred, Alvin, Oscar, John, and I showed him Ben's February letter and shared ideas and possible strategies. We asked him to be our negotiator and to use his skill and contacts to help free the kidnapped men.

A towering figure, six feet seven inches tall, Terry Waite exuded energy and quiet confidence. In six years as the Archbishop's special emissary, he had scored several negotiating successes. In 1981 he traveled to Tehran, obtaining the release of four British citizens held by the Iranians. In 1984 he succeeded in gaining the freedom of four Britons held in Libya. Now we were asking for his help for Ben and the others.

John and I spoke briefly to him alone, grateful for his willingness to pursue the matter. Terry stressed that he had no political point of view and worked strictly from a humanitarian perspective, always mindful that those who engage in desperate acts have suffered themselves and need to be treated with respect as fellow human beings. He was firm that he could not represent our government but wished to be a neutral mediator.

Several days later we all met again with Terry Waite, this time at the presiding Episcopal Bishop's apartment. Ollie North flew in from Washington to join us. He greeted us warmly but appeared harried and intense: the Administration was doing everything possible; if the kidnappers wanted money, money was not an issue. After Ollie left, Terry spoke to us in general terms. Ever discreet, he guarded confidences jealously, but he appeared hopeful and ready to act on our behalf. It seemed we were making progress at last.

On May 15 I was startled to see Ben's picture flashed on our TV screen, along with pictures of Father Martin Jenco, Terry Anderson, William Buckley, and two French hostages. Ben had on an old sweat shirt. He was clean-shaven—no beard this time; even his head was shaved. The pictures looked like typical shots of prisoners. Some of the men looked glum. Ben's expression was serious but he looked all right.

Islamic Jihad had sent the six pictures to a Beirut newspaper, along with three statements: one addressed to world opinion, another to the Rev. Jesse Jackson, the third to the families of the hostages. Surely this must be in response to the Rev. Jackson's full-page appeals that we had sent to four Beirut newspapers a month earlier. At last we had reached the captors themselves!

The statements included the following passages:

> We assure you that we are not kidnappers and obstructors of freedom just for the fun of it, and it is not our nature to practice aggression against others, but we are a small community of tormented people who suffered a great deal of misery at the hands of the aggressors the United States. . . . America has executed against us the most atrocious crimes for the purpose of national security and other times under the pretext of fighting against terrorism and for human rights; with the end result of our being the victims paying the price with our own blood. . . . America and her agents do not understand any language but the language of force. . . . Raise your voices . . . and help us release the hostages detained by us. . . . Peace in the world cannot be imposed by force.

Following the release of these statements, the Rev. Jesse Jackson accompanied members of the hostage families to the State Department.

Unable to get an appointment with Mr. Shultz, we met with Robert Oakley. Rev. Jackson said he was prepared to go to the Middle East if he could meet with the American hostages. Asked later about Rev. Jackson's effort, Bernard Kalb said, "We are prepared to facilitate such private efforts, if requested. However, those persons undertaking such private initiatives do not speak for the U.S. government."

The demands of Islamic Jihad were depressingly difficult to carry out, but at least the pictures were confirmation that Ben and the others were still alive.

One month had gone by since our meeting with Terry Waite. We heard indirectly from the Administration that three of the seventeen prisoners held in Kuwait were about to be executed. That meant that three of the seven hostages might be killed in retaliation. Archbishop Runcie invited Alvin to meet him in London to discuss the involvement of Terry Waite, so Alvin made a quick trip to London. Subsequently it was agreed that Terry Waite would work full-time for the release of the hostages.

On June 14, TWA Flight 847 from Athens to Rome was hijacked and finally landed in Beirut. One American serviceman was killed and the 152 remaining passengers were held hostage. The Shiite hijackers demanded the release of the seventeen prisoners in Kuwait. Many of the passengers were released, but thirty-nine Americans continued to be held on the plane.

This time the Reagan Administration treated the taking of hostages as a crisis and began negotiations. Finally, after seventeen days in captivity, the Americans were set free.

During those seventeen days, the families of the seven other men held in Beirut hoped their men would be a part of the negotiations. But when I asked this of Robert Oakley at the State Department, his response was depressing. "You wouldn't want to delay the release of the thirty-nine for the sake of your husband, would you?" It was heartbreaking that an opportunity to resolve *our* hostage crisis had been missed.

The hostage families were becoming better organized. California Representatives Mervyn M. Dymally and Robert K. Dornan sponsored a "Forgotten Seven Awareness Day" in Washington. We held a press conference and a discussion with members of Congress. Robert Oakley at the State Department was there, along with Oliver North. As usual, we were assured every possible effort was being made for the release of the men.

The next day we met with Mr. McFarlane in the situation room in the basement of the White House, escorted by Ollie North. John opened the discussion by saying that the families wanted to cooperate with the Administration, but the release of the seven was urgent. Someone asked if the crusade through media and Congress was the right thing to do. Mr. McFarlane paused for several seconds. "We understand your frustration," he said. "Go right on doing what you are doing."

The Administration seemed very nervous about our relationship with the media. After our meeting was over, we were told, "Those who do not want to meet with the press can go out this door, but the reporters are going to see you if you go out that door." We went out to meet the reporters. We told them we were grateful for the meeting but we felt additional actions needed to be taken, including direct dialogue with the captors. And we still were seeking an appointment with the President.

It was now three months since we first saw Terry Waite. Early in August, Alvin, Fred, John, and I flew to London for another meeting. This time he sounded hopeful that at least some of the hostages would soon be released. He told us he thought Ben would be one of them.

In the middle of August we met with Oliver North in his office in the Old Executive Office Building. I had read in the newspaper that Colonel North had been involved in drafting a letter on terrorism from President Reagan to Syrian President Hafez al-Assad that had angered President Assad. Was this true? I asked. We needed President Assad; he had been helpful in freeing the thirty-nine. North said he was not the sole author of the letter and, in fact, had acted to "tone down" its wording. He continued, "I am a believer in the Lord Jesus

Christ, and I have dedicated my life to him." I responded, "I am also a believer in the Lord Jesus Christ and I have dedicated my life to him, but I may disagree with you."

That summer Dennis Benson and Gregg Hartung of the Presbyterian Media Mission came to us with creative media ideas to keep the hostage issue before the American people. These two broadcasters wrote and produced a series of eight television spots with composer-writer-comedian Steve Allen. More than 250 stations ran these public-affairs messages, which were commissioned by the Presbyterian Church (U.S.A.) and Catholic Relief Services. John and I were present when the spots were taped in Los Angeles. Mr. Allen's willingness to give of his time and talents on behalf of the hostages meant much to all of us.

The months dragged on. There had been so many meetings, so much discussion without any change. I became more aware of what seemed to me to be the silence of God. What was happening to Ben during these long months? When would this nightmare end?

We ourselves had tried to stir the Reagan Administration to take new initiatives. We had made many private and personal appeals. I remembered the story in scripture of the widow who had knocked and knocked on the door of the unjust judge, the judge who cared nothing for God or man. Finally, because of her persistence, the judge responded. I felt like that widow, whose story has been told over and over for two thousand years. I was knocking on many doors in Washington. Would one door finally open for Ben's release?

Later I was to learn from Ben that he, too, read that same Bible story during his captivity. He had interpreted it to mean that God does not object to our repeated petitions.

Perhaps God does not speak but remains silent to listen for something in us. Perhaps God listens for openness and receptivity on our part to the creation of a new, fresh spirit.

21

"You are the one chosen."

Toward the end of the first week in September, the Hajj came and sat on a mattress in our room and began talking with us. As usual, I served as translator.

He said that the guards were considering the possibility of releasing one of us and asked which person we would choose to be freed. The hostage would need to convey a message to the U.S. government to put pressure on Kuwait for the release of the men held there, and he should also try to convince the American public to press their government to become more active in responding to the demands of the captors.

The Hajj did not spell these matters out clearly. We told him we would need some time to talk it over.

When he came back the next day, we said that Terry Anderson, the AP correspondent, would in our view be the best choice. The Hajj didn't seem very impressed by our decision; he seemed to think someone else would be better, but he didn't say. We did not know whether or not to take his remarks seriously, although for us it was certainly a serious matter.

As the days passed, we began to think that nothing would happen. Then one evening, without prior announcement, the Hajj appeared. As usual we were all blindfolded. The guard, Said, was with him. The Hajj said it had been decided that I was to be released that evening.

"You mean right now?"

"Yes, you will be released right now."

"Well, I would like to go, but are you sure I am the one who is most helpful and most in need of release?"

"You are the one chosen."

"If you want someone to take a message, Terry Anderson is more capable because he is a newsman and has connections. If you want someone who needs to be released, I think of Father Martin, who is not in as good physical condition as I am."

"No, you are the one who is going to go," the Hajj responded firmly. "You will have your beard trimmed by Said, you will take a shower, and then you will go."

I remember exclaiming out loud, "Oh, God! What can I do?" I translated the Hajj's announcement to the other hostages. They were dumbstruck but quickly congratulated me. I sympathized with the deep yearning of each one of them to be free. For my part, I wanted to live and return to my family; I was glad. But at the same time I was in deep consternation. Could I do anything to bring about the release of my brothers? I doubted that and felt helpless. But there was no time to reflect.

There was nothing left to say. Said came in immediately and trimmed my beard. As he worked, I thought of how I had never had a beard before being taken captive. I didn't like it, but at that moment I determined to wear it until my fellow hostages were released. It would be a way by which I would continually remember them and perhaps remind others that there could be no rest until these men were free. I took a shower and then hugged each of my companions in a tearful farewell.

Said ushered me out of the room. I was wearing only a well-worn jogging suit and a pair of rubber slippers, in addition to my usual ski mask. As I started down the stairs, Said shoved a wad of paper in my pocket: notes the men had written to their families while I was getting ready. At the bottom of the stairs I was led to the back door of a car and told to lie face down on the seat.

The Hajj sat in front, next to the driver. As we went along the road, he said to me, "You are to do two things. First, tell the American government that they are to put pressure on Kuwait for the release of the men being held there. Second, say that you have been released as a sign of our good intention of solving this situation, and to do it quickly and without publicity."

I said, "You mean on behalf of the other hostages?"

"Yes, all five of them."

He said that William Buckley was the other one. I had never seen him, but I had heard his voice; he had been kidnapped in March of 1984, two months before me.

After twenty minutes or so, the Hajj said, "Be ready now to get out of the car when it stops. Take off your ski mask as you step out, and don't look back. You will know where you are."

Shortly after this the car came to a stop. I took off the mask and climbed out, and the car sped off. I found myself on a familiar street in Beirut near the university. It was around midnight, and the street was deserted.

I immediately went to the home of friends. Then I got in touch with the American Embassy. They were not expecting me; all this came as a very great surprise.

The next day a vehicle came for me with four armed men. Quickly I got in, and we were off on a wild ride through West Beirut to the eastern sector where the embassy was now located. As I sat down between two men with submachine guns, the one on the right handed me an automatic pistol, saying simply, "Use it if you need to. Flip off the safety with your thumb, like this"—and he demonstrated.

After that there was no more talking, except for the man on the radio. We careened over the major boulevards at breakneck speed, each looking to his own side for trouble, and I looking to both sides. There was only occasional traffic. Soon we reached the western edge of the no-man's-land that separates West Beirut from East. Instead of going straight ahead over the usual route, we headed south, outside the western wall of the large racecourse, and then dashed through a gate in the wall.

That took us on a narrow, winding dirt road through the racecourse. One man with a shoulder-fired RPG—rocket-propelled grenade launcher—could knock us out at any minute, I thought. But we left the racecourse behind without delay, entered the eastern sector, and sped down the old Damascus highway. Another sad thought gripped me: I may be seeing these familiar streets for the last time.

At each major intersection there was a vehicle with one or two armed men waving us on. They were expecting us. Inside our vehicle, someone would say with relief, "They're our guys."

Neither the tension nor the speed slackened, until finally we climbed the steep slope to the embassy, were admitted by the security guard, passed through the barbed-wire perimeter, and came to a sudden stop at the entrance to the embassy building.

I was ushered in like a foreign dignitary (but wearing borrowed clothes) and was introduced to the Deputy Chief of Mission. He was most cordial, offering me food and drink repeatedly and offering me Ambassador Bartholomew's office to rest in until the ambassador arrived. Sandwiches and soft drinks were provided, and I was given the freedom to wait in the ambassador's office or stroll in the enclosed veranda on the side of the building. The staff was always with me. Food and drink were offered again and again. I walked around and talked to the security people. There were guards everywhere. I was very much impressed by how tight and extensive the security was. The staff kept apologizing for having to make me stay in the embassy. I said, "Look, this is freedom to me. It's a whole new situation just to be able to walk around the room without a chain."

The Deputy Chief of Mission and several men on his staff were curious to know how I had been released. Obviously they were surprised at my good condition. After an hour or so, the ambassador appeared, saying he had left an important engagement, all smiles and congratulations over my appearance. He said that there was hope that one or more other hostages would be released soon.

I told them I wanted to call my wife, but they said, "There is no possibility of doing that." I was not sure what that meant, so I asked to call one of my daughters, either Ann in Egypt or Chris in Saudi Arabia. They told me that my daughters had gone back to the States. I said again that I wanted to get in touch with my wife. Ambassador Bartholomew said any publicity at this point would be injurious, and the government felt it would be best if Carol and I were secluded for a few days. When I asked about my wife and family, he assured me they were well, but that publicity might prevent the release of additional captives. He said the plan was to fly me to an aircraft carrier for a few days, awaiting any possible further release. I agreed, saying I would accept that limitation if it was only for a few days.

They were delighted. I was told they would fly me out by helicopter. However, it would take several hours to get the aircraft here. The ambassador had some appointments, so he left. He didn't want to arouse public suspicion by not fulfilling his other commitments at this time. He had been very cordial, but he had little information to convey.

For the next several hours I jogged in his office and did some exercises. I looked at a couple of magazines. There was a small screened portico with an outside garden. I walked in the portico and admired the natural growth that filled it. It was amazing to see green plants after such a long time in the dark.

Finally, in the middle of the afternoon, they took me out of the embassy with marines and other guards all around me. I was surprised how protective they were. I was being treated like someone special.

A large helicopter had landed near the embassy. I climbed aboard, and we headed west toward Cyprus. On board, I met a few officers from the carrier, who said they were prepared to return to Beirut if an additional hostage should be released. I was given a green airman's flying suit and told to buckle into a bucket seat. The noise prevented much conversation, but obviously it was a friendly crowd.

Perhaps an hour later, as we landed on the flight deck of the U.S.S. *Nimitz,* I was handed a flight helmet and told I would appear as a member of the flight crew, to avoid all publicity.

I was led directly to the small hospital area without talking to anyone. There, medical personnel took care of my personal needs and gave me a thorough medical examination, which resulted in a clean bill of health from both the physician and the psychologist.

Only at mealtime did I leave that area briefly, being led to the officers' wardroom and back again. Several times, apologies were offered for such tight restrictions, but for me this was more freedom than I had known for 495 days, and I knew now that confinement would be short. Part of the time was spent in debriefing concerning my captivity.

On the second day I was told that soon I would leave for the United States. No additional hostage had been released, but there was still hope. Would I agree to proceed to a secure area in the States where I could be alone with my family for a few days while they were waiting, out of the public eye?

I countered with a question: "What does Carol think?"

I was told she was agreeable, depending on what I wanted. So I agreed to the suggestion, understanding it would last only a few days more.

That evening I donned a flight suit with helmet and parachute and boarded a small plane that I was told was a submarine hunter. We were catapulted off the flight deck into the late-afternoon sun, headed toward the air base in Sicily, where I transferred to a C130 cargo plane that offered space to walk and sleep.

A doctor accompanied me on this leg of the journey. When I asked why he was coming along, he said that he had been ordered to stay with me until I reached the States. This tender, loving treatment was in sharp contrast to my experiences in captivity.

There was never a more welcome sight than the lights of the East Coast of the United States. We landed at a military airfield in Norfolk, Virginia, about midnight on Monday, September 16. I had expected that my family would be there, but only a couple of men wearing civilian clothes came out to the plane. They greeted me with one or two words and then took me into a lounge area, where Colonel North, several CIA people, and a nurse were waiting. They too congratulated me on my release and apparent good state of health. I gave thanks to God for his sustaining care throughout the 495 days of my captivity.

They said they wanted me to go to a "safe" place, and I replied that I wanted to see my wife. Colonel North said that my family was in a Norfolk hotel. Very good, I said, I want to see them. He kept advising all of us to go to this "safe" place that was ready for us. He stressed the importance of being out of the public view.

I insisted that I would only make that decision after I talked with my wife. I repeated this until finally the colonel agreed that I would be taken to the hotel to meet my family, although he didn't advise that we stay there. I said I would make up my mind after talking with them.

I was introduced to Dr. Bullard, a psychiatrist working with the State Department, who said that he and the nurse would go with me to the hotel. We got into a car with one or two other persons. On the way there were more expressions of gratitude and surprise about my release and good health.

We arrived at the hotel in the early hours of the morning. Dr. Bullard took me out of the car and up by the back stairs, carefully avoiding a stop at the front desk. We went down the hall to a door and knocked. Was Carol on the other side of the door? Who else was there? How had they changed? How would they look?

The door opened and there stood Carol. There was a look of pure amazement on her face. We hugged and kissed. I hugged each of the three children who were there—Chris, John, and Sue. Ann, I learned, was coming from Egypt. I was delighted to see Fred Wilson, a former classmate, who was there with Alvin Puryear. Oscar McCloud would be arriving the next day.

Carol had obviously expended a great deal of energy during the last sixteen months. She was exhausted. Although she was excited and happy about the reunion of the family, I could see what a heavy toll it had taken. I know her so well and this whole role of getting up front, being aggressive, being public about everything, assuming an extrovert role created unbelievable pressure on her.

Our son and daughters showed great maturity. I was very moved to learn how well John had supported his mother emotionally. Not only had he stuck by her, he had aggressively moved forward on my behalf, where he might well have surmised that it was a hopeless situation and done nothing. Chris had seen opportunities for using her knowledge of the Middle East, her Arabic, and her connections in imaginative ways. Sue had been keen on strategy and organization, and Ann had been equally supportive. The whole family had come together in this crisis. They complemented each other, worked together, spoke out on my behalf.

It was wonderful to be back.

22

"Your husband has been released."

It seemed as if Ben's release would never come. We had just about exhausted all our ideas.

On Sunday, September 15, 1985, I was taking part in the worship service at a small church in Iowa. The minister was in the middle of her sermon when someone came in and told me I was wanted on the telephone. I can vividly remember the blast of the minister's amplified voice as I took the call. It was the White House. I was asked to wait because they wanted to connect me with my daughter Christine in California and with Mr. McFarlane.

I waited. What news were we about to receive? Mr. McFarlane came on the line and said that he was sorry to disturb us. I said, "Don't worry about that." He paused and said, "Your husband has been released." He immediately added that they thought this information should not be made public. At the White House, they were only going to say, "No comment." He said, "We can't control you, but we would like to ask you not to release this news, because we think some other hostages might be released in the next day or so. We don't want to do anything to jeopardize this possibility."

I told him this was wonderful news, thanked him for telling us, and immediately asked when we could see Ben. He said Ben was aboard the *Nimitz*, in the custody of the U.S. Navy, and would be flown to Frankfurt. His release to us would take five days. I asked to talk to Ben on the phone, if I could not see him. I was told this was impossible. I said the family wanted Ben to go to Geneva, where he could be out of the public eye. Mr. McFarlane thought this might be possible; he would let me know.

I canceled my plans for that afternoon in order to fly to New York. I was publicly asked about the story that had appeared on television about Ben's release. I hated to do it, but I said there had been so many false reports we could not get our hopes up. I wanted to be open with them and rejoice over the good news but felt I should follow Mr. McFarlane's wishes.

The church official of this presbytery flies his own plane, so he flew me to my connection for New York. Reports from the Middle East about Ben's release had already started to appear.

Chris phoned Sue the good news. John was at the airport, about to leave on a long-scheduled trip to New York, when Christine got hold of him and told him too. He was being pressed for answers by the media people surrounding him at the phone, so he and Chris spoke Arabic. She told him to abide by the Administration's request and not say anything.

More reporters met John when he changed planes in Chicago and when he arrived in New York. He did give a few up-close interviews to press people who had been helpful and covered the story at the beginning when no one knew about the hostages, but he assured them that he knew nothing. Then he and Fred Wilson met my flight.

Later that night, hiding at an airport motel under Fred Wilson's name where no one from the media or from the government could find us, we discussed where we wanted to meet Ben.

For months the Administration had promised us that if Ben was released they would abide by whatever arrangements we made. We had left suitcases with clothing and shoes in Damascus and Beirut for him. Now we were told they did not want Ben released in Geneva; they wanted him returned to the States.

They started giving John and Fred a hard time: one State Department official even called Fred and said that he was coming to stay at his house that night. Fred finally called the White House in protest.

Colonel North told John they had this great "safe" house, where the family could meet Ben and the press couldn't get at us. He tried to convince us that this arrangement would be best for us all.

At this point we were in a state of paranoia. We were as concerned about being locked in as we were about the press being locked out.

After consultation with church and family, we decided that we did not want Ben or ourselves in a safe house. I really wanted to meet him when he stepped off the plane on American soil as a free person.

In the morning, John telephoned Colonel North that we had agreed to meet Ben in the States. He was very happy. He said they needed to know our decision so they could direct the flight carrying Ben, but as we learned later, he was already on his way before John called.

We insisted that Ben be delivered to us. They agreed and said they would provide transportation for us from LaGuardia Airport to Norfolk, Virginia, where the plane carrying Ben would land.

All this time they kept admonishing us to say nothing to the press.

They even accused us of leaking the news, until John reminded them that the dateline on the story was Beirut. We were asked not to mention Ben's release for three days, in hopes that other hostages might be released. We agreed. We were told that if we did not cooperate they would blame us, if other hostages were not freed. It was amazing that we had gotten everyone into New York without anyone's knowing where we were. We thought we had done a great job of living up to the Administration's request for secrecy.

Our party included most of the family plus church officials Oscar McCloud, Fred Wilson, and Alvin Puryear. Ann would be coming in from Egypt in a few hours. We left in a leased unmarked aircraft from a deserted part of LaGuardia, and we landed not at any of the large military airfields but at a deserted airstrip outside of Williamsburg, Virginia. There was no tower. A fire truck came out on the field. As soon as we were down safely, everyone involved with the flight disappeared. The plane flew away and the truck drove off.

Three government station wagons were waiting for us. The drivers wore dark glasses and did not seem to have names. They would not identify themselves or show us any identification. They said they were going to take us to the safe house. We said we had decided to reject their hospitality and had made reservations at a hotel. We asked when Ben would be getting in and when we would be seeing him. They had no answers to our questions.

There was quite a discussion. They claimed they didn't know how to find the hotel, but we were firm. Fortunately, Alvin was from the Norfolk area and promised to show them the way.

They had to phone someone for permission, but it was finally agreed that they take us to our hotel. Along the journey the government people questioned us about whether this was the right decision or not. They said they couldn't protect us from the media in a hotel.

We wanted Ben alone. Nothing would move us from this latest agreement with the National Security Council. We had originally planned to have him to ourselves for a minimum of one month. We had read about how confused and disoriented prisoners like this often are. We had no idea what shape he would be in. John had lectured me about how prisoners in isolation play mental games to keep alive and may have a hard time learning to relate normally to people again.

When we were settled in our rooms, we learned that all these government people were suddenly going to be staying there also. The party included the drivers, a psychologist, CIA agents, and a woman companion who was there to give us comfort.

We were not very inconspicuous: five men and three women surrounded by eight government agents with dark glasses, radios, and raincoats. The agents would not let us go into the lobby, so John Nelson signed us all in as "Wilsons."

We took our meals in our rooms and waited. Colonel North phoned that Ben was supposed to come in at 11 P.M. He was still unable to convince us to go to the safe house.

We rented cars so we could pick up Ann when she arrived and be there to meet Ben's plane. We waited and waited. The time for his arrival was long past.

John called Colonel North. North was surprised that we had not heard from Robert McFarlane, who was supposed to be in touch with us. Reached by phone, Mr. McFarlane told us that Ben was now coming in at a different field. It was too far away for us to get there by the time his plane landed. I was upset. I said I wanted him to get us to the airport where Ben would land. "That is up to you to arrange," he said. But it was too late for us to make such arrangements. Surely he would not want me to tell the press that Robert McFarlane was keeping me from being with my husband? Mr. McFarlane started out in a controlled voice, telling me that the government had spent millions to get Ben released. He accused me of being difficult and ungrateful. Finally he shouted, "I'm tired of you, young lady!" and slammed down the receiver.

John used a special number to call Mr. McFarlane back but was told by the switchboard operator that Mr. McFarlane was not available to him. We tried to get hold of Colonel North. How were we to meet Ben? Finally, the White House duty officer told John that Ben would be delivered to the hotel shortly.

It was now two in the morning. I was discouraged, nervous, and testy at not being allowed to greet Ben as he landed. Why couldn't they have arranged a telephone call to him at least? What were they going to do with him?

There was a knock on the door and there was Ben! He looked quite a bit older. He had a beard, his hair was whiter, and his face was very pale. We embraced and then he hugged the others, one by one. But in the midst of our joy, I was still upset that I hadn't been allowed to meet him at the plane.

23

"What can we do?"

The family looked just the way I remembered them. We spent hours catching up on the details of our lives. I learned how the government had managed to get us all where they wanted us to be. Sue, who is particularly sensitive to the way government works, was pleased that I had not agreed to go into some kind of seclusion. We did decide to continue our news blackout. If anyone knocked, I would be careful to step out of sight.

Having a bedroom and a bathroom seemed like a whole new experience. Just being able to get a glass of water when I wanted it seemed like a miracle. Freedom was wonderful. But the real wonder was being reunited with my family.

It was hard to put everything together. The narrative thread just wasn't there. My story came out in bits and pieces. I had a lot to tell —and they had a lot to tell. I wanted to hear their stories, too. I was only beginning to learn of the enormous effort Carol and the family had made on behalf of all of us. We finally decided to pick everything up the next day, and we fell into bed. I was deeply thankful to God for this reunion and for all his sustaining grace throughout the past sixteen months.

On Tuesday we continued our feast of storytelling and sharing. Ann arrived from Egypt. She had a different hairstyle and seemed to have changed more than the others.

Wednesday morning we had a call: the White House wanted to speak to Benjamin Weir. I went to another room. A navy operator said that in twenty minutes the President would speak to me from his plane, Air Force One. I said fine, because I had a message to deliver to him from my captors. The man told me that when Mr. Reagan was on the phone I was not to use his name or refer to him by any title. "You can only use the code name 'Rawhide.'" This really struck me funny. I couldn't believe what I had heard.

Twenty minutes later the phone rang and President Reagan was on the phone. He said he was so happy I was safely back with my family. He had been praying for my safe return. He went on in this vein without a break. I realized that if I was going to deliver my message from the kidnappers, I would have to break into the President's speech.

I was not going to call him Mr. President if they didn't want me to. But I certainly was not going to call him "Rawhide." He was calling on an open line and everybody was listening in; there was no need for code names. I just said, "I have a message I want you to hear. First, my captors have told me that they expect you to put pressure on Kuwait to release the seventeen men being held there. Second, they want me to tell you that I have been released as a sign of their good intention to resolve this issue."

There was no response. He finished reading whatever had been prepared for him and hung up.

President Reagan had mentioned in his statement that it did not look as if the others would be freed, so if I didn't have any objections he would announce my release at twelve forty-five that afternoon. I said that was up to him. Since he was saying there was no longer a need to keep my release secret, we went ahead and announced a press conference for Thursday at the National Presbyterian Church in Washington.

Fred Wilson reported that people in government were asking for a debriefing, and I agreed to meet with representatives of the FBI and the CIA at the hotel. I asked Alvin Puryear to go with me for this debriefing session, because I wanted a sympathetic observer and witness. My questioners hedged a bit at the beginning. Some of their questions could only be asked in the presence of a person with security clearance. To their surprise, Alvin assured them that he does a lot of consulting with government agencies and has clearance.

I was disappointed by the unsophisticated questions, much like those I had been asked as I left Beirut: "What was the food like?" "What were the health conditions?" They wanted to know about the location of the places where I was kept and the identity of my captors. I was afraid they might try to rescue the other prisoners by force, so I refused to say anything that might endanger them.

We spent several hours at this—most of the day, in fact. Alvin and I felt that the information probably wasn't much help to them. We also insisted this should be the only debriefing. The FBI contacted me several times in the coming months, but I refused to undergo questioning again.

Because we were not going to make any comments to the media until our press conference the next day, we slipped quietly out of the hotel to shop for the clothes I would need. Carol and the girls were meticulous in deciding which tie would go with which shirt.

Meanwhile, I learned from Carol what a press conference was and how one should have a statement to read at the opening. By Wednesday evening I had written out what I wanted to say and knew what I did not want to discuss.

The staff of the National Presbyterian Church and Center placed the entire facility at our disposal. I was grateful that the press conference could be held there. As I left Beirut, I had worried about how I was going to deliver my captors' message and arouse concern for the remaining hostages. But when Carol, Alvin, and I walked into the church sanctuary, there were 200 international media people present to hear me. The church was the right setting, and the crowd was in a receptive mood. Many even clapped when I came in.

The questioners were friendly too. Former hostage Jeremy Levin of CNN was one of them, but I didn't recognize him. I felt a very strong sense of mission. I appreciated all the people who had worked on my behalf, but it was also very important to me to give thanks to God publicly.

I was on the evening news live with Dan Rather of CBS and Tom Brokaw of NBC. ABC broadcast an interview by Peter Jennings. The next night I was on PBS. Then followed a whole series of network shows, arranged by Marj Carpenter of our Atlanta office.

I was still stunned by how much care and concern, prayer and praise, came out of my experience. Carol's efforts on my behalf had made much of this happen. She was backed up by Fred and the Program Agency. Yet it went far beyond the love and care of the Presbyterian Church. Many other people were supportive of me and my family during the whole time of my captivity.

After the press conference came my chance to meet the family members of the other hostages. I had heard so much about them during my last months in captivity I felt that I already knew them, and I hugged them all in turn: Father Martin's sisters, Mae Mihelich and Sue Franceschini; John Jenco; Eric, Paul, and Diane Jacobsen; Peggy Anderson Say and Glenn (Rich) Anderson; Jean Sutherland's Tom and her youngest daughter, Kit; Rose Kilburn, wife of Peter's nephew Tim, and niece Patty Little, among others. We also welcomed Elaine Collett and her son, Karim. She is the American wife of British subject Alec Collett, the UN correspondent in Lebanon who was kidnapped in March 1985. And of course Jerry Levin and his wife, Sis, were there.

All the families sat in a circle, and I spoke in detail about the four men I had lived with for two and a half months. In addition I gave them the hastily written notes that had been stuffed in my pocket the evening I left. I was able to tell each family member that I had lived with their loved ones and they were all in good health. For the families it was the first time they had had any direct communication from the men, let alone the chance to talk to someone who had actually been with them. It was almost like a message from the living dead.

It was an emotion-filled gathering. "What can we do?" they asked. I felt their task was, first, to keep the hostage issue before the American public and, second, to support the efforts of Terry Waite, the special envoy of the Archbishop of Canterbury who had been working as a mediator.

24

"Let Carol put it on your finger."

It was unbelievably good to be back together again. I reviewed our long journey of the past sixteen months: so many miles, so many calls, so many visits, so many pleas to bring Ben and the other hostages safely home. In the last few hours of this nightmare, we had even had to struggle to set Ben free from our own government!

The State Department and the National Security Council did not seem to share information. If they had worked together—and if they had just had some feeling for us as a family—it would have been so much easier for us. Instead, we got the impression from the Reagan Administration that if the hostages were sacrificed, it was just too bad. We felt that these men weren't really persons to their government but were more like soldiers, expendable for the cause.

In all the confusion, we had had very little time alone. Friends, reporters, church people—everyone wanted to hear our story. A great burden had been removed from my shoulders. No longer would I wake in the morning, immediately remembering the awful fact that Ben was a captive in Lebanon. Now it was time to resume our life together.

The Program Agency arranged for us to go on a cruise in the Caribbean as a vacation. We needed time to relax and talk, and a cruise was the perfect setting for this kind of sharing.

In St. Thomas, we went shopping to replace the wedding ring that one of the captors had pulled from Ben's finger. We were able to find a band that fit, and the saleswoman asked if she should put it in a box. Ben said he wanted to wear it. He started to put it on, but the saleswoman stopped him. "Let Carol put it on your finger," she said. So we restored the symbol of our life together there in the jewelry store.

Will I ever see Beirut again? There is a refugee family living in our apartment, which we left fully furnished. At the request of a neighbor, the young woman there was glad to send along a few of our personal belongings. There seems to be a bridge of understanding between individuals even as the destruction and pain caused by opposing political forces continue to swirl around us.

I learned many things during those two years, in the course of my unexpected journey. I learned that people of faith are not entitled to special privileged rescue from the trials others are subjected to. I learned that the Reagan Administration was reluctant to meet Ben's captors in face-to-face negotiations—perhaps afraid to lose its macho image, perhaps afraid to confront the reality that our foreign policy in the Middle East has been misguided for so long. I learned anew about the strength of the faith community, the church, as I compared the government in Washington with the body of Christ. There is so much potential there!

The binding and freeing of Ben has helped me learn that worship and politics are closely related. Both opportunities for participation raise the same question: Whom shall we love and whom shall we serve? The answer is staggering in its simplicity: our neighbor. And who is our neighbor? The global community. For God loved the whole world.

25

"Peace."

On the morning of July 31, 1986, in London, I opened the door to the office of the Archbishop of Canterbury. The Archbishop was talking with another man who had his back to me. He said to him quietly, "Father Martin, a friend is waiting to see you."

Father Lawrence Martin Jenco turned around. It was five days after his release. We held each other at arm's length for a few seconds and then embraced. It was a tearful, joyous, emotional hug. He said to me, simply but repeatedly, "Peace."

I responded with feeling. "I'm deeply thankful that the Almighty has delivered you. Praise God."

On Sunday night, November 2, 1986, Carol and I were in a hotel room in Puerto Rico when the telephone rang and a reporter told me David Jacobsen had just been released. Wonderful news! We knew how much it would mean to his family, especially his son, Eric, who had worked so hard.

I was unable to meet David when he arrived in Washington, D.C., but once home in Los Angeles he phoned me. I thanked God for his release. "Ben," he told me, "we've got to work for the release of Terry and Tom. Someday soon the 'church of the locked door' will become the 'church of the open door.'"

Since the day I was set free from my physical captivity, life has become a miracle and an adventure. Every day is new. The gifts keep appearing. An unexpected flower, the magic of a telephone call from a family member, an airplane ride to another city, the privilege of talking with friends and strangers, a sound night's sleep and a healthy body, the closeness of family, the exciting joy of public worship—these are truly presents from the gracious Creator and sustainer of life.

As I enjoy the beauty, security, sensory stimulus, and emotional warmth that surrounds me, I am aware hour by hour of the two deprived men who were left behind in Lebanon. Terry Anderson and Thomas Sutherland—these are my brothers in Christ for whom I pray. I want to do whatever I can to promote their freedom. Yet at the same time I surrender them to God. I ask repeatedly that his goodwill be accomplished in their lives. May they know inward peace and be able to trust in his Spirit who is present with them. *Please deliver them from bondage, God.*

I know how hard the wait is for their families. It is frustrating not to be able to communicate with these hostages or know what to do that will bring about their release. The spirit of forgiveness of the Kilburn family toward the captors who killed Peter is especially moving. Such love says something profound about obedience to Christ and the possibility of learning to live together on the same planet.

I have also seen at close range the weariness, the frustration, the unswerving commitment of Terry Waite to do everything in his power to negotiate the release of the remaining hostages. In spite of ambiguities, discouragement, and personal risk, he has pressed on. From him I have gained a deeper appreciation of the unique role of the church ecumenical.

Life is divinely given. Each person is to be respected and deserves to be heard. The captors themselves need to be set free. We are all recipients of God's mercy and forgiveness. On that basis we can begin to trust each other and find the constructive things we can do together as Muslims and Christians.

What a time to engage in Christian mission! While we become advocates for the homeless, the unemployed, the disenfranchised, and the discouraged within our own borders, we are called to look beyond our own society to the world and its needs. Faith lets you know that you can't just stand back and say, "I'm not here," hoping the trouble will go away. We must learn to live together.

In November 1985, Ben and Carol Weir flew to Egypt to be with their twenty-four-year-old daughter Ann, who was a teacher in the Schutz American School in Alexandria. Ann and her friend Kathy Lorimer, also the daughter of missionaries, met Ann's parents at the airport, and there was a happy reunion at the Lorimer home. Ann gave her parents the presents they were to take with them and open at Christmas. That evening the two young women boarded a bus to return to Alexandria. On the way, the back of the bus was struck by a train, and Ann and Kathy were killed.

In January 1986, San Francisco Presbytery nominated Benjamin M. Weir, one of its minister members, for the highest elective office in the Presbyterian Church (U.S.A.), that of Moderator of the General Assembly. When the Assembly met in Minneapolis the following June, Ben was elected over three other candidates. At the reception honoring the new moderator, Ben and Carol stood together, hostages once bound, now hostages free.

In November 1986, Ben Weir received the following telegram:

Dear Reverend Weir:
I was saddened to learn from press reports that you may have accepted at face value speculative stories in the media alleging arms for hostages. Let me assure you that no ransom was paid for your release. The long-standing policy of our government has been to make no concessions to the demands of terrorists. I firmly believe in that policy. To do otherwise is to encourage additional acts of terrorism and place many more Americans at risk. All of the extensive efforts your government has undertaken to obtain your release and the release of all the other American and foreign hostages in Lebanon have been fully consistent with that policy. My efforts to protect our broader interests in the Middle East and to achieve the release of the remaining American and other foreign hostages will and must continue. I know you agree.
                                                    Ronald Reagan

Ben has said, "I would be deeply saddened to think that my freedom was at the expense of further escalating the terrible warfare between Iran and Iraq."

CHRISTIAN HERALD ASSOCIATION AND ITS MINISTRIES

CHRISTIAN HERALD ASSOCIATION, founded in 1878, publishes The Christian Herald Magazine, one of the leading interdenominational religious monthlies in America. Through its wide circulation, it brings inspiring articles and the latest news of religious developments to many families. From the magazine's pages came the initiative for CHRISTIAN HERALD CHILDREN and THE BOWERY MISSION, two individually supported not-for-profit corporations.

CHRISTIAN HERALD CHILDREN, established in 1894, is the name for a unique and dynamic ministry to disadvantaged children, offering hope and opportunities which would not otherwise be available for reasons of poverty and neglect. The goal is to develop each child's potential and to demonstrate Christian compassion and understanding to children in need.

Mont Lawn is a permanent camp located in Bushkill, Pennsylvania. It is the focal point of a ministry which provides a healthful "vacation with a purpose" to children who without it would be confined to the streets of the city. Up to 1000 children between the age of 7 and 11 come to Mont Lawn each year.

Christian Herald Children maintains year-round contact with children by means of a *City Youth Ministry.* Central to its philosophy is the belief that only through sustained relationships and demonstrated concern can individual lives be truly enriched. Special emphasis is on individual guidance, spiritual and family counseling and tutoring. This follow-up ministry to inner-city children culminates for many in financial assistance toward higher education and career counseling.

THE BOWERY MISSION, located at 227 Bowery, New York City, has since 1879 been reaching out to the lost men on the Bowery, offering them what could be their last chance to rebuild their lives. Every man is fed, clothed and ministered to. Countless numbers have entered the 90-day residential rehabilitation program at the Bowery Mission. A concentrated ministry of counseling, medical care, nutrition therapy, Bible study and Gospel services awakens a man to spiritual renewal within himself.

These ministries are supported solely by the voluntary contributions of individuals and by legacies and bequests. Contributions are tax deductible. Checks should be made out either to CHRISTIAN HERALD CHILDREN or to THE BOWERY MISSION.

Administrative Office: 40 Overlook Drive, Chappaqua, New York 10514
Telephone: (914) 769-9000